CARIBBEAN

INNOCENTS

A Thirty Year Love Affair
With Bequia, Jewel of the
Windward Islands

By

Patricia T. Fischer

Illustrated by

LouLoune

Penfield
Press

DEDICATED TO

Karl, my love,
who has made life an exciting journey.

THE AUTHOR

Karl and Pat Fischer

Patricia Fischer is a graduate in communications from the University of Iowa, Iowa City, Iowa. She lived with her attorney husband in a small town, Vinton, Iowa, until his retirement in the early 80s. She currently divides her time between Bequia, St. Vincent, Grenadines, West Indies; Naples, Florida, and Bovey, Minnesota. She and husband Karl maintain their masterpieces are their children: daughter Betsy, who lives with husband Rick Hadley in Vinton, Iowa, and son John and wife Michelle of Cedar Rapids, Iowa. The Fischer's grandchildren are: Ross and Nori Hadley; Jenna and Ian Fischer.

ILLUSTRATOR LouLoune lives on the island of Martinique, Grenadines, West Indies. A graduate of "Arts Plastiques de Paris," she has had many exhibitions on the islands and in Paris. Her paintings on silk and her watercolors depict Caribbean life and legends. She illustrated the book *OKA,* in order to include "Amerindians" in the "Heritage of Humanity."

ASSOCIATE EDITORS: Dorothy Crum, Joan Liffring-Zug Bourret, Melinda Bradnan, Dwayne Bourret
GRAPHICS EDITOR: Walter Meyer
COVER DESIGN: Kelly Behrends Hughes
To order by mail, postpaid: *Caribbean Innocents,* $14.95, from: Betsy Fischer Hadley, 115 Scenic Drive, Vinton, IA 52349
(Iowa residents add 5% sales tax.)

CONTENTS

Editor's note: Names in some of the stories are fictional.

 BEQUIA ISLAND is the northernmost and largest of the Caribbean islands known as the Grenadines. Succeeding the Arawaks, *Becouya,* in the Carib tongue meaning "Island of the Clouds," was occupied by a native Carib tribe. For most of the 17th and 18th centuries, the French, British, Spanish, and Dutch disputed over the agricultural riches of the islands. The Caribs repelled these forces well into the 18th century. Eventually France and England tired of fighting and the Caribs began to yield to pressure. A series of treaties finally gave possession of St. Vincent and the Grenadines to England. Prosperity on Bequia attracted many British subjects, as well as families from Scotland, France, and other European nations. Divided into a number of estates, the island's economy thrived until the abolition of slavery in 1838. A decline in production, as well as population, characterized the last half of the 19th century.

In 1979, the State of St. Vincent and the Grenadines, including Bequia, gained independence within the British Commonwealth. Today, Bequia is famed as one of the few unspoiled islands left in the world. Many visitors have built winter homes in the tranquil, seafaring atmosphere.

PART I

DISCOVERY

SQUALL

The sky is blue nearest the sunrise.........
But across the inky waves
A squall line comes in
So that sheets of rain appear
Against the mountainside

Giving the hibiscus and bananas
A welcome drink.
Only for a moment.
Then......
The rain is gone........
And the sun glistens
With the promise of another day
Of peaceful perfection.

March 11, 1967

BEGINNINGS

In the dark of an Iowa night, I awakened cold — my dreams were of some of the things my husband, Karl, and I had experienced on the tiny Island of Bequia in the southern Caribbean. They weren't world shaking events. I guess you might call them the "passing through" kind of things — ones that someone says, "You should write that down. It's such a good story you should remember it."

So, I got out of bed, conjured up that emerald island and starting writing about it.

How It Began

Whenever Karl and I are introduced to most anyone as the owners of a plantation on the Caribbean island, they shake their heads in wonder as they query, "For heaven's sake, how did people from a little town in Iowa get way down there?" This is the story.

In 1963, Karl's brother-in-law and sister, Dudley and Margaret Taylor, chartered the eighty-six-foot yacht "Dixie," to go diving with their children in the lower Caribbean. As a contractor it was necessary for Dudley to take his vacations in the winter and important that he take them first class and where there was good water for scuba diving. The Dixie had just come over from the Mediterranean and the skipper had enlisted a young Bequian, Basil Lewis, to teach him about the water in the Windward Islands. He soon established himself as the man to have around when the family was diving. He was a great free diver, going down ninety or so feet without a tank, unheard of in northern waters. He knew the good diving waters, as well, locating the best reefs, the most colorful fish and the largest lobsters.

When Basil suggested his grandmother made ice cream on Saturday night, it took little urging for the skipper to turn the tiller toward her house on Bequia. Gem of the Caribbean, tiny Bequia, seven by one and a half miles, is the largest and most developed of the Grenadines, a chain of islands stretching southerly from St. Vincent some fifty miles to Grenada. Highly regarded, since the 1700s, as a vacation spot for white aristocrats, Bequia's flat, undulating lands were suitable for agriculture, and its excellent and safe anchorage served the seafaring people, boat builders and whalers, of the island and New England. Whales passed Bequia in their annual migration from the north and those whalers knew a good thing when they saw it — forget the chilly waters of the Atlantic for whaling in the sunny Caribbean. When we arrived on the scene, they were still pursuing whales with their little sailboats and using hand-held harpoons. (Although they seemed to be fortunate to get as few as three or so a year.) Whatever they caught fed the families of Paget Farms in the south of the island. The red meat was corned or salted to preserve it, and the blubber was rendered into oil for shipment abroad.

In the center of the island was an enclave of Scots, descendants of political refugees from the time of Mary Queen of Scots. For the most part, though, the residents today are an interesting mixture of African and European ancestry, from many places in the world and with traditions as varied. By 1963 the island had gained renown among sailors as one of the safest and most beautiful harbors in the

"In the center of the island was an enclave of Scots, descendants of political refugees from the time of Mary Queen of Scots."

Caribbean. Not only was it in the midst of the best sailing waters, but diving in the Grenadines was marvelous.

So Basil and his party went ashore in Port Elizabeth to visit Grandma. There Dudley, always aggressively social, soon learned who was who on the island and what was what.

I must digress to tell you that since the days of Karl's cruise to Trinidad and Tobago in 1943, as a midshipman at the U.S. Naval Academy, he had dreamed of returning to what he thought was a tropical paradise. When Dudley and Margaret had started their invasion of those waters, he jokingly implored them to find a little piece of an island for his retirement — and in that vein, for sure.

With Karl in mind, Dudley asked the same questions he had been asking in the northern islands for the past three or four years, "What about land here for homesites?" He learned from the Lewis' none was being offered then, but that Cecil McIntosh, a fourth generation descendant of the Scots on Bequia, wanted to go to England for his health; that he had a plantation there on Bequia and was dickering for its sale to Anthony Eden (Lord Avon, a former prime minister of Great Britain). Dudley also found out that Cecil's prospect wasn't moving towards the asking price fast enough, and he was unhappy with the negotiations.

Cecil's plantation, called "Spring Estate" for generations, was about 270 acres on the northeast side of the island. The Lewises said it was beautiful: that Cecil lived in nearby downtown Port Elizabeth and that they'd take Dudley over to see him about his problems. Within hours the latter was drinking fruit juice on the McIntosh veranda, listening to the neurotic Scot tell about his ailments and need to get off the island for medical care. After the tour of illnesses came the tour of Spring Estate. Dudley and Margaret were enthralled.

By the time the Dixie weighed anchor several days later, Dudley had established the purchase price for Spring at $10,000 more than Anthony Eden would finally bid. And he then had entered into a very loosely drawn contract with the sick man for the acquisition of the estate…, "a little bit of land for Karl."

Next, Dudley sent a cable to Karl, then in the frigid northland drudging a living in the prosaic things small town attorneys do to make ends meet. "Come inspect Caribbean plantation you have just purchased. Reply requested. Dudley, Dixie, Kingstown, St. Vincent." Karl's response was swift: "Dudley, go to hell! Karl."

But when Dudley and Margaret returned to Iowa with pictures of Spring, Karl was convinced the matter needed investigation. It was then that he put the bite on my father, John Tobin, an Iowa Circuit Court judge, Walter Newport, an old attorney friend, and Keith Elwick, president of a local manufacturing company, to venture into the southern Caribbean. The purpose: to see what Karl had bought and what he should do about it.

So it was that four intrepid Iowans boarded a United Airlines flight…final destination Bequia, St. Vincent, West Indies, someplace close to Trinidad and Tobago. The same evening they reached Antigua, sixty degrees warmer than Cedar Rapids, Iowa, with a full moon glistening on English Harbour. Hey, they agreed, this is lots better than our unmelted snow and leaden skies. They were already hooked.

The next morning, as the group flew to St. Lucia from Martinique, Keith turned to Karl and asked, "What do you suppose that stuff splashing off my window could be?" Karl gulped, called a stewardess and watched her run to the pilot's cabin. A quick return to the Martinique airport gave the

*"The captain was so loaded with rum
they were concerned about a safe landfall."*

answer. A workman had neglected to replace both main fuel caps after fueling. Nearly all of the high test gas had been siphoned from the tanks. Unbeknownst to the future owners of Spring Estate, they had just observed one of the characteristics of the Caribbean that would drive them close to madness.

The passage from St. Vincent to Bequia on an overloaded island work boat under sail was another learning experience. The captain was so loaded with rum they were concerned about a safe landfall.

Paradise was found on Bequia. None had ever seen anything as beautiful as the harbor at Port Elizabeth at sunset. Rowing to the sand beach, they were met by youngsters who directed them to someone who would lease them a house on Tony Gibbons's beach. By the time the kids had rowed them to that beach in a boat designed to handle half that many, night had fallen hard, as it does in the southern Caribbean.

The four barefoot itinerants stumbled, without light, up the hill from the beach to the house that was there someplace. It was found more by feel than by match-light. Once there, Karl's main concern was to find the bathroom to relieve a greatly distended bladder. He felt his way gingerly along a wall leading to the back of the house where he located a room presumed to be the toilet — it was the shower. And something large, furry and nameless started running back and forth over his feet. His bloodcurdling shriek could be heard for miles.

Matches enlightened the foursome. Karl had cut off the escape route of a manicoo (possum) that had entered the shower through the drain hole. During the brief encounter, each was trying to find his way out. Escape was made at about the same time.

Tapers were located and the adventurers found straw ticks on the floors that were to serve as beds for the remainder of their visit.

By eight o'clock snores abounded in the small house. About two a.m. Karl was awakened by moonlight streaming across his face. He padded to the front door, only faintly lighted. A second scream of the night aroused everybody else. This time it was a human animal. Walter had preceded Karl to the porch, and each appeared out of the shadows unrecognized by the other! The rest of the night was spent oohing and aahing at the moon glistening on the bay.

Next morning the four tourists inquired at the "People's Store," the only grocery on the island (consisting of open air cupboards with doors open during store hours), as to a place that would furnish breakfast. An hour or so later, replete with eggs and local sausage from a seaside kitchen, they searched out the Cecil McIntosh residence.

The McIntosh bungalow sprang from a garden center of tropical color. Therein, though, was the pasty-faced and colorless lord and master of Spring Estate, who acknowledged the group with solemn mien. After explaining his lot as a sick man, he volunteered to take them to his estate and summoned help from a young man, Harold Wallace.

Harold was the owner of the "LuluBelle," a run down Land Rover without a generator and without brakes. Somehow it had survived the junk pile. The vehicle proved to be one of three cars on the island. One of the others was up on blocks behind the Sunny Caribbee and was owned by Tom Johnson who was then managing that hotel. The other was owned by Noel Agar who was in some stage of considering the construction of Friendship Hotel in the south end of the island. Harold, Cecil, the four tourists and two teen-age pushers, used in lieu of a starter for the car, journeyed over Thomas Hill for Spring.

Eight-hundred years earlier the Arawak Indians from South America had found Spring Estate. Its bay then was surely ensconced by hills of white flowering cedar, frangipani and wild cinnamon as it was when the American foursome saw it. Toward the sunrise, the fringe of coral sand fingered out into crystal clear water that was nearly waveless to the outer limits of the bay, a staghorn coral reef. The volcanic rock of the bay's headlands on the north rose in stark majesty, only agave and cactus breaking its monotony. The hills on

the south of the bay were covered by windswept greenery —
not a residence anywhere.

In the amphitheater of hills behind the bay were fields of
pigeon peas overgrown with wild tamarind. In the valley
were citrus and mango trees badly in need of pruning and a
grove of banana trees that appeared abandoned. In the flat
land back of the beaches were acres of eighty-year-old
coconut trees that formed a canopy over the coconuts lying
helter-skelter on the ground below.

At the foot of the hills there were plantation buildings in
a state of final decay. There was a "great house" with rotted
floors and a rusted through red tin roof; its only trace of
grandeur being an arched stone stairway and flagstone patio.
Set into the patio was a sundial with a date noting first occu-
pancy of the house — 1776.

Since Spring had been a working sugar plantation until
long after slaves were freed in 1833, there were the sugar mill
ruins — the crushing shed with a sluice running to cauldrons
under which fires were kindled to reduce the cane syrup to
sugar. Only the old chimney was left intact though, the
remaining coppers lying about rusted and unusable.

To the rear of a rusted-tin-roofed shed, bananas were
hung for ripening. In the same building Cecil showed the
party a sad reminder of slavery days — a dungeon hardly
high enough for standing, with slatted iron doors, one small
window, and rusted manacles still secured to one of the walls.
(Soon after we signed our final contract of purchase the manacles were chiseled out of the walls and stolen.)

Even in its run-down condition, Spring Estate was a place
of raw beauty. One could dream of that which it could be.
The decision of the inspectors was mutual and immediate. It
confirmed the purchase Dudley had made but included a

"LuLubelle"

piece called "Salt Petre" that had been excluded when Dudley dealt with Cecil. With the glitter of gold in his eyes, Cecil sold his birthright to the foursome on a five-year payout with an option for the buyers to pay sooner. A young St. Vincent attorney was employed to draw the contract of sale and to assure the buyers that there were no problems connected with the sale. Well, maybe one small problem.

Non-resident aliens were required to make an application to the government for an "Aliens' License" to hold land in St. Vincent, including the Grenadines. "But," said the lawyer, "that should be no problem. Such licenses have been issued as night follows day." After the contract was signed, he was authorized to make the necessary application. The foursome then returned to the States.

Four weeks or so later Karl got a letter from our attorney with the application for an Aliens' License. It was short and to the point. All of the people applying were held in esteem in their own communities. No reason existed why the license should not issue.

It was a month later that the bomb dropped. Karl got his second letter from the attorney: "The ministers have flatly and unanimously denied your request for an Aliens' License."

In retrospect it was a reasonable decision they had made. For years the islands were rarely visited. Getting there from anywhere before the airline arrived was a function of the few wealthy enough to spare both the time and money for travel by yacht. Then the airlines brought many people, some who considered buying land for speculative purposes, and the latter usually had money. Speculation drove up land prices so local people couldn't afford homesites. The result was bad for the island, bad for the politicians.

Anyway, the news was then devastating to Karl. He

hopped a plane for St. Vincent the morning after he heard from his attorney. "What are we going to do? Cecil has already spent our down payment of $80,000."

"The prime minister will see me tomorrow, Mr. Fischer. I'll see what he wants!"

The next day: "He says he wants you to institute some kind of light industry on your estate. People over there need work." Karl told our lawyer there was no way his people were going to be operating an industry on Spring, 2,600 miles from Iowa. He then told him he had clients with businesses right across the street that weren't properly managed and that he (the lawyer) should ask for an alternative.

A day later: "Mr. Fischer, he says he would go for a hotel of at least ten rooms."

Karl flew back to Iowa with the message. The foursome met and decided to pursue the feasibility of the alternative. A young architect of some note in Cedar Rapids, and a former professor at Iowa State University, Ray Crites, was a shirt tail relative of Keith Elwick's wife. Keith suggested Ray be consulted about the matter. Ray was interested and so was Dick McConnell, his partner. Dick, too, had been a professor of architecture at Iowa State. They were both super bright and innovative and were looking for a challenge. (Later the two changed the face of the campus at Iowa State with many buildings of their own design.)

At about the same time, Walter Newport decided that "the practice of law is a jealous mistress" and opted to get out. Karl took his share. Dudley decided he should not screw up his credit with a loan on a "goose chase," and my father took his share. The architects decided to participate for stock.

Leaving the Judge in Iowa, Karl and I, Keith and Janet Elwick (Keith's wife), and the architects gathered passports and headed for Bequia. The architects were excited; Karl and I...a little apprehensive. Up to that point the two of us, as it was later on, were furnishing all of the funds for the project.

While the Julian McIntosh band pounded out calypsos on the veranda of the Sunny Caribbee, the Iowa entrepreneurs were considering what could be done to comply with the conditions imposed for an Aliens' License. The next morning two young black men sought out Ray Crites on that same veranda. They said they were the best builders on Bequia, that they had been contracting roads mostly but could build anything we needed. Thus it was that the McIntosh brothers, Julian and Basil, began their long association with the owners of Spring Estate. Julian was then twenty-six years old, with an eighth-grade education and, unbeknown to the innocents planning how to build a hotel, was to become responsible for the development of a multi-million dollar enterprise that would span decades and change the lives of hundreds of families on Bequia.

Oh, how to build a hotel in the Caribbean with all of the principals 2,600 miles away in Iowa! Karl, Keith and Ray all knew they needed some kind of representation in the building process: somebody should check construction in progress and verify labor performed and material purchased. That somebody should have experience in building. A search was commenced.

Klaus Alverman was a young German architect hand building a sailboat (with which he later sailed around the world) on the waterside in Port Elizabeth. He was also designing a beach house for a man we met at the Sunny Caribbee, Gus Koven, the new owner of Hope Plantation on the lower windward coast. Gus assured us Klaus could be the man we needed for our project, and Ray employed him to do those limited things we had considered. He also asked him to advise Julian with respect to minor matters that might arise because of the latter's limited experience.

Plans for the construction of the hotel were completed and an estimate made of the cost. Karl was advised, borrowed the money in his own name and deposited the proceeds in an account established in the Royal Bank of Canada. Julian could draw on the account only after Klaus had verified the labor performed and materials used. The account would not need additional funding until eighteen months or so, the target date for completion.

Four months later, Karl got a cablegram from the manager of the Royal Bank: "Please wire funds to cover overdraft." A telephone call to the manager disclosed that indeed, our funds were finished.

Klaus had found that the walls of the old great house we were depending upon to hold up the second story of our hotel were glued together with a mortar made of ground coral fired in manchineel, both materials then found on our estate. The trouble was that the so-called mortar had biodegraded and, in effect, our stone walls would not be stable or strong enough to hold another story of stone. So, Klaus told Julian to tear down the walls, go deeper with the footings and rebuild. When Ray and Karl returned to Bequia to see the problem, the walls were just where they were when they left.

Karl: "Ray, how much is it going to cost now?"

His response: "You know the answer. The same as it was when we left."

Shades of Teddy Roosevelt sending the fleet halfway around the world without funds for its return.... We, like Roosevelt's congress, were an unfriendly bunch required to provide funds to get the fleet back. Karl borrowed some more, again in his own name.

With only a thousand or so minor crises, Spring Hotel was completed in February of 1968. We arrived in time for the traditional celebration, when the brightest of oleander branches was tied to a pole and attached to the highest peak of the new building. Julian's wife, Isola, and family had made dozens of sandwiches and side dishes. With plenty of beer and rum, the workers' party was just short of all-out drunkenness, a joyful ending to a long tribulation.

Spring Hotel was nestled into a hillside. There were three bedrooms, kitchen, bar, and a canvas covered outdoor dining room in the main building; only one bedroom in the old summer kitchen, and two more in the old servants' quarters. Then there were two bedrooms, attached as a suite, with a living-dining room and kitchen, in a fortress-like stone building; there was another bedroom with the same amenities in a stone building looking like the first. All had private bathrooms with showers and gas lights used in those days aboard ship. Still on the drafting board was a stone four-plex.

All of the hotel rooms were paneled in purple heart, and all roofs were of thick-butt wallaba shingles, both woods from Guyana. Ray Crites had spent days in the archives of Martinique to find the design for our roofs. The combination was to be the model for West Indian construction up and down the island for the next twenty-five years.

Morning cold showers were warm by midday; the generator driven filter gave our swimming pool a sparkle, and the tennis net had not yet been eaten by goats. The Caribbean prints of our bedspreads and chair cushions lent color. Straw floor mats softened the flagstone floors.

Our hotel was no longer a nightmare, but a beautiful dream come true.

"Please wire funds to cover overdraft."

Part Two

So we returned to the ministers and said, "See, here is the ten-room hotel you required of us as a condition to hold Spring Estate. Now, please grant our Aliens' License as you stated you would in your letter outlining that requirement."

And the ministers said, "Ah, yes, we know about the letter. But we are a newly elected administration, and we are not bound by the last one. Your Spring Hotel is a good start. Construction has provided work and pay for many families over a long period, but that hotel only occupies a small portion of Spring Estate. We want a plan for the acres left. We suggest a development."

Our hotel architects recommended that we consult Jim Shive of Cedar Rapids about considering subdividing the rest of the estate. Jim, head of a very good firm of civil engineers that had experience in planning such things, even in the Caribbean, readily agreed to fly to Bequia to see the problem firsthand. He did his spade work from Spring Hotel.

Jim had aerial photos taken of Spring and, with them in hand, returned to Cedar Rapids. There he used computers to make topographical maps from the photos. (The British did the same thing in later years.) With those maps he subdivided three of Spring's hills and made a presentation to our group showing the lots he proposed. Each was serviced by an old, cart road that appeared on the aerial photograph, was less than one acre, and would have an unobstructed view of Spring Bay. He had had an opportunity to examine some of the cart roads to be used when he visited Spring, and recommended that making them useable would be duck soup. The shareholders were sold.

Jim flew back to Bequia to implement his plans by surveying an addition we would call "Old Cart Road," and Karl borrowed more money in his own name for the project.

The survey proved to be more time consuming than Jim had estimated. Cutting brush and hardwood trees was not the same as softwood counterparts in the States. Finally completed, though, he took his plan of the survey to the Department of Lands and Surveys in St. Vincent. "Mr. Shive, it appears that you have a proper plan for filing, but we need your registration number as a surveyor. Without it, we can not accept the plan."

Jim was aghast. He had been filing plans in the northern islands for years and reciprocity had always been granted. Well, it wasn't a given in St. Vincent. Jim, sure that another civil engineer on the island would help him out with a signature, asked for a list of surveyors in St. Vincent. "Mr. Shive, all of our surveyors are off the island at the moment on projects of one kind or another. Leonard Sandy has just finished a job in Canada, but he's looking for another one up there."

Jim convinced Mr. Sandy to return to St. Vincent on the condition that he resurvey the whole plan. So it was that we were double-charged for "Old Cart Road." But, then, Mr. Sandy surveyed another hill of ours we called "Crown Point," filed both plans and handed them to us for presentation to the ministers. The Aliens' License was finally granted. More money was borrowed in Karl's name and Cecil McIntosh was paid in full. Spring Estate belonged to the shareholders of a Vincentian company formed by our group called "Always Spring, Ltd."

Slowly a small residential colony began to form in the hills of both of the new subdivisions. Roads were hand-hewn with pick and pecks from the mountainous terrain and finished with two strips of concrete strengthened by re-rod.

Jim Shive had laid out the division of another of our hills by computer, and had run survey lines through the bush there. He had not finished the plan for the reasons mentioned. Although Leonard Sandy had gone back to Canada, the owner of a travel service in St. Vincent told us her husband, Stinson Campbell, might be convinced to help us finish. Stinson was a registered surveyor and indeed, he was willing. We fed and boarded his crew for three months or so at Spring Hotel while they made the survey. He took it to Planning for approval.

"Since your latest subdivision began, Mr. Fischer, the United Nations implemented a committee to help developing countries in planning real estate projects. We now work with a board of that committee based in Barbados. We want that board to review your project and approve it or make recommendations for changes."

My God! We'd had it again. This time it took nearly a year before the engineers at Barbados got to examine our plan on site. "Mr. Fischer, some of your roads are too steep." (All Canadians, they were concerned about any road over ten degrees in grade — ice, you know, in Canada.)

Mr. Campbell spent another month on ferries from St. Vincent to Bequia and back redesigning roads. Some were later abandoned as impractical. But Planning approved, "Pea Patch" was filed and roads were built. Now, where were the buyers? Definitely not on Bequia!

"Mr. Fischer, some of your roads are too steep."
(All Canadians, they were concerned about any road over ten
degrees in grade — ice, you know, in Canada.)

ON TO BEQUIA

It may be that somewhere on this old sphere there is some bigger "wheeler-dealer" than Karl Willard Fischer, Esquire, but I sincerely doubt it. When Pan Am sent our luggage on to Trinidad last night at midnight, he disrupted the whole Caribbean transportation system. All Bajan Pan Am employees were up all night, and at 7:30 a.m., there was a call to report that the return plane (jet, that is) had left Trinidad an hour early so as to connect with our LIAT flight. Now, how Pan Am notified the hundred-odd jet passengers of the early take-off, we'll never know, but as Dorris just remarked, "Karl, you're the only person I know who could commandeer a jet and not do it illegally."

Everyone was most cooperative. The officials at Cedar Rapids cleared the twelve-foot curtain rods with all of the air carriers from there to St. Vincent. The LIAT officials at Barbados though, reneged. They said it couldn't be done in their little air frames. There was a difference of opinion. Karl assured them that it could. Guess who won? Right. They must have taken that LIAT plane apart to get them in — but they got them in somehow! The curtain rods extended from the rear seat to the front seat, under the seats, next to the side.

The doors closed on our flight to St. Vincent and the engines were revved up. Then I discovered my gaily bedecked flight seat had been left behind at the gate. I needed that seat — bad back. Karl implored the pilots to let him out, and they did. He tore back to the gate, retrieved the seat and conned the luggage handlers into giving him a ride back out to the plane. (In the meantime, I had been standing in the doorway of the plane so they couldn't shut out my husband and take off.) On to St. Vincent with candy, Orange Ju-C, and the curtain rods.

Getting the curtain rods into the plane was one thing.

"Hero Karl tore out to prevent the take-off."

Getting them out was something else. The St. Vincent baggage handlers said it couldn't be done. The pilots, who hadn't been privy to the operation when they went in, were of the same opinion. While Karl was involved with customs, I watched the debate with great interest. Then, after about twenty minutes, the pilots decided they'd had enough of this tomfoolery and would take off with the rods. I reported their decision to Karl.

Since we'd already brought the rods 2,600 miles, Karl and I couldn't go with that decision. Hero Karl tore out to prevent the take-off. The end result was that the rods were removed through the windows of the pilots' cabin. As the engines were again revved, the captain pulled open his window and roared, "That's the last time I'll do anything nice for anybody!"

PART II

HAPPENINGS

BEQUIA FISHING BOATS

The fishing boats go out
With a lantern at the bow.
And the flicker of light across the waters
Joins the flicker of stars in the heavens.
Early in the evening for bait,
Early in the morning for fish.
Full-sailed they appear on the horizon
To enter the harbor in mid-morning sun.
Muscle and knowledge and courage and skill —
Men of the sea.........generation after generation.

March 7, 1966

SPRING BEACH PICNIC

It wasn't as if anyone needed an excuse for a party, but the combination of palm trees, Caribbean breezes and a full moon made it an opportunity not to be ignored. So the word went out on the island's grapevine (there were no telephones or radios) about a party .

Just before sunset the group gathered at McIntosh's. How did they get there? Well, there were no taxis on Bequia in 1966...only two cars and a van and none of those belonged to our people at SPRING. Out there we had something different. What our transportation lacked in sophistication it made up for in character. The SPRING tractor had been pressed into service and hitched to it was a huge flatbed wagon. Forewarned, someone was equipped with a torch (flashlight) which would satisfy the local constabulary taillight requirements after night fell.

Our arms loaded with supplies, we piled onto the wagon. Up Thomas Hill we chugged, over the crest and down onto the windward side, arriving at SPRING beach in plenty of time to start a cheery coconut husk fire.

I don't remember how or when the McIntosh contingent arrived, but I know their transportation was much safer and more reliable than that of the vacationing white Americans. So they took charge...still letting us be a part of things, but knowing the answers we had yet to learn.

Julie's ready smile reassured us we were in good hands. The director of the production was Isola. It was her first of many over the years. All afternoon her kitchen helpers had

"What our transportation lacked in sophistication it made up for in character. The SPRING tractor had been pressed into service..."

been frying chickens and baking bread, as well as preparing banana and coconut fritters for dessert. (The latter would be sprinkled with brown, island sugar, and lime juice before being popped into our salivating mouths.)

Early on, the moon rose making pathways of silver across the water. The silhouette of the palm trees, the soft lapping of the waves, the sky full of stars, the gentle trade winds, our coconut fire, all made an ambiance most of us had never seen before. One could almost hear the sighs of pure contentment.

Of the many things we learned that night, one was about Mt. Gay rum. On the rocks, or mixed with ginger or water, it enlivened the pace of a beach party — a lot!

I don't remember eating...though I do recall the sea grape leaves we gathered to use as platters for sliced tomatoes and chicken. My memories are more of the beach people that night.

First of all there were Julie and Isola...keeping it all on an even keel...enjoying themselves, but never quite succumbing to the flow of the party. Lillian, Isola's mother, was there. She had to be convinced to attend at all, and was still shy with the gregarious Americans. But after enough rum, even Lillian and her friend were dancing by the fire, showing us Bequia rhythms as they sang familiar calypsos.

The rum "spoke" that night. Kay Shive, sitting beside me in the firelight's shadows, laughed as she listened to her husband, Jim, sing thirty verses lauding the "Cherry Point Light"...a sea chantey dragged up from memories of youthful beach parties on the New England coast. "He hasn't sung that song since Navy days. He refuses to sing...ever! I can't believe it." Yet, sing he did, dancing around the fire as he rendered his own version of a calypso. Rum had broken a stolid engineer.

Some of us were more conservative. Bob and Barbara Ferris, Janet and Keith Elwick, Karl and I hadn't yet gotten into the swing of the Caribbean. That came later on.

Two who knew the ropes were Ruth and Barb. Veterans of trips to other Caribbean islands, they discovered Bequia at about the same time we discovered them. At the time, they were perched on bar stools during the cocktail hour at the Sunny Caribbee. They were fun and bright, and we immediately adopted them as important members of the "Spring" family. Ruth, a blonde, was the Registrar at Bradley University, while Barb, a brunette, managed the University bookstore which served the many facets of life on campus. My memory of that night is of a conversation overheard as they peered into an empty thermos which had sheltered gimlets a short time before...with a challenge to refill the thermos to provide enough gimlets to finish the party. Ruth, pouring gin onto the ice, observed, "We've used up all the lime juice. What shall I do?" And resourceful Barb, seriously appraising the situation, countered, "Not to worry...just fill it up with gin." That's exactly what they did the evening of the party. Those gimlets were perfect.

I mustn't omit Herb, our estate manager at the time. Herb, straight from the chill winds of Iowa, was on his first trip to the Caribbean. As a conservation officer and the former manager of a fast food restaurant, he'd had the experience that could have been helpful in many ways in the Midwest, but his skills were utterly useless in Bequia. His first mistake was to leave his wife behind in Iowa. It was she who managed and led. Without her presence, Herb was a lost soul — was afraid of the natives — was afraid to stay alone at Spring. He was in a state of concealed panic most of the time. Because the beautiful purple heart doors on his room were so heavy and impossible to close in the wind, and since one whole side of Herb's bedroom consisted of those doors, he couldn't stay dry when the driving rains commenced. So, when we arrived at the Fort to keep him company, he had commandeered a huge piano crate from somewhere. It was practically serving as his bedroom and was littered with cigarette butts and bits of paper. He was pleased to have us there, and by this party night he was ready for anything.

Demon rum was just *that* to Herb. He'd not had a drink since 1946 when, as a serviceman in World War II, he'd discovered his incompatibility with alcohol, but good company and a moonlit night made Herb forget. Janet and I commented early on that we'd never seen him like that before. An hour or so later we met again by the fire when replenishing our rum punches. "Janet, how's Herb getting along?" "Gosh, Pat, I haven't seen him lately. Come to think of it, though, the last time I saw him he was staggering toward the sea with a bottle in his hand."

Suddenly sober, we put out the word and everyone fanned out to search the shallow water and beach area. We carefully avoided deeper water where we'd been warned sharks might lurk during the nighttime hours. No Herb — anywhere! Fatalistically, we decided nothing could be done until morning, but the party was definitely over.

Then it became necessary to find out "who will ride back with Keith on the wagon?" No one! Keith had been the heaviest of the imbibers, although he was ordinarily not much of a drinker. Finally loyalty triumphed when Janet and Bob Ferris volunteered to keep track of him. As Karl and I walked up the hill to the Fort, we watched the light of the tractor snaking its way though the coconut groves till at last it disappeared over Thomas Hill.

Oh yes — and Herb? Well, next morning we found him - safe and sound in his packing-box bedroom. He sheepishly admitted that, at some time during the party, he had realized it was necessary to get up that hill to bed. Since everyone seemed to be having so much fun, he decided not to bother anybody about his departure. He had crawled on his hands and knees through the palm groves, across the banana patch, past the old great house and finally up the serpentine strip road to security and bed.

It was a marvelous party! One to remember!

THE SUNNY CARIBBEE

In 1946, just following the disaster of World War II, Sydney McIntosh, one of the heirs to the old plantations of northern Bequia, decided the island needed a proper hotel. By the time we arrived in 1963, he had built the "Sunny

Caribbee," and it was in operation as the welcoming landfall for travelers visiting the island.

Of its two stories, the first was built of stone Sydney appropriated from the old sugar mill on brother Cecil's "Spring Plantation." The rape of the old ruins was not then considered a crime and the stone was all cut and easily available. The second story was of hand-sawn lumber taken from the hills of the plantations Sydney and Cecil owned on the island. On the first floor, there was a large kitchen, a dining room and a huge "el" shaped veranda, at least twenty feet in width, that extended to an enormous flamboyant planted many years before construction. The veranda served as both lobby and lounge. In the corner hung a large rope hammock, perfect for napping or reading. The wooden chairs were all of local design, painted white and sported colorful cushions.

Toward the sea from the hotel smaller napping hammocks were hung among a cluster of cedar trees. Deployed among the hammocks were planters' chairs whose white arms could be extended forward for sunning and relaxing (the Caribbean chaise).

The top floor consisted of a wide hallway that ran east and west, with ventilating means on each end and rooms on both sides. The one bathroom was located on one side of the east end, near the stairs.

During the day the bathroom proved adequate for both overnight guests and those visiting the dining room. But the pumper who filled the water tank for all of its needs went home at 8:00 p,m., so anyone fulfilling the urge, from the hours past about 2:00 a.m., found the flushing water finished until the pumper returned to duty at 7:00 a.m.

Each room had a skeleton key that locked the door. In addition, there was a long, heavy hook anchored to the inside of the door near the lock that served two functions. It could be used to hold the door open and kept the door from slamming in the wind. Hooked open, the doors served as ventilators for the breezes running through windows blocked up with wooden stakes.

In 1964 one experienced romance as a guest of the hotel, notwithstanding its total lack of sophistication. It was a getaway, but its managers had a different perspective. It was one big problem. No electricity. No telephone. No engines. A rusted kerosene freezer stood in a convenient corner of the dining room. Sometimes it worked, sometimes it did not. Many times guests would find it lying upside down, one of the means of rejuvenating the monster.

"The ice was brought by boat from St. Vincent..."

Cooking was done in the primitive kitchen on either bottled gas stoves or local charcoal cooking pots. Water was pumped by hand from the cistern. The icebox was filled daily. The ice was brought by boat from St. Vincent in large burlap covered blocks. From the dock it was taken to the hotel by dinghy.

The hotel had many managers from the time we first knew it. The first was a couple from Chicago fleeing from advertising, Tom and Gladys (Glady) Johnson. They were bright executives and applied their ingenuity with vigor. After several years they purchased land on the south end of the island and developed it very creatively, naming it "Moonhole." Their home was carved right out of the volcanic rock of the area. It is so unique that it draws architects, builders, and sightseers from all over.

Of the other managers, the Palmers were outstanding. Jan and Gerry were scions of highly regarded St. Vincent families. They knew the territory, had management ability and coped. The hotel prospered, but the Palmers were looking for bigger things and went to Mustique. There they managed the "Cotton House" for Colin Tennant (Lord Litchfield). The latter was a descendant of the Tennant family, England's premier brewers, and was developing the island as a prestigious vacation spot for the rich and famous. He made it.

After thirty years we have nostalgic memories of the Sunny Caribbee. We became close friends with many of its employees. The young girls then are grandmothers now. More than a few of them worked for us at Spring Hotel over the years. But we saw most when we stayed there while they were doing their daily chores: making the beds, letting down the mosquito nets, supplying punks for the under-the-bed mosquito repellents, lighting the kerosene lamps and, most of all, as waitresses.

Most of the employees of the hotel were tentative. None

had been trained in their respective lines of work until their employment at Spring. No one in the kitchen thought to boil water early enough to give it time to cool before mealtime. It was always brought to the crock boiling hot where precious ice was used for immediate cooling. Portions and quantities were added not multiplied. To make enough for eight, two portions of four were made.

All food was local and fresh. Recipes were local. The product was delicious. I still use those recipes for Bequia puff, fish pie, tannia fritters, callaloo and pumpkin soup, lime pie, rum cake and penny rolls.

There were other managers of the hotel. Mike and Phyllis Sprangue were tempted to give it a try and left their New England to do so. My recollection is that Mike was a friend of Tom Johnson at Princeton. They stayed for two years, long enough to become disenchanted with paradise. Then came Sally Littler, a former airline stewardess. Sally was young and pretty. After a few years she sailed south to assume the managerial duties of the "Nutmeg" that then had a reputation as the place to go in Georgetown, Grenada. Chester Peters, the skinny little boy who had rowed Karl by dinghy from the dock to his rented home on his first trip, became one of the later managers. It was good to see someone we'd known for so long find the pinnacle.

Listening to the then managers recount their trials and tribulations was a large part of the entertainment for the guests. And it probably made the managers feel better. Anyway, the stories were usually incredible, even though factual.

The constant nocturnal barking of dogs and the crowing of roosters was a part of the hotel scene. Years in the Caribbean have proved the nuisances to be universal there.

Jump-ups for hotel guests on the veranda were weekly occasions. From the time of our first visit, the pan band of the McIntosh brothers played those jump-ups. The four brothers were all musically talented and formed the core of the band. The other members were also talented but changed from time to time. The steel drums for their pans were heated, pounded and tuned by the brothers. Handmade quatros and guitars formed the string part. As time went on, the band broke up. Patrick became an Anglican priest; Leo, the head cook on a tanker; Basil, a master stone mason. Julian, the leader, became the leading contractor on Bequia, the manager at Spring and, with his wife Isola, our closest friend.

From our harbor-facing room in the hotel we watched the fishing boats from Hamilton put out to the bay at midnight. With kerosene soaked torches on the bow, they seined for bait the rest of the night, coming in for early breakfast. Then, at daybreak, out they sailed to the open sea, fulfilling their roles as fishermen.

Occasionally, in our beds we could hear the clip-clop of hooves on the quarry tile of the lobby; some donkey had pulled loose from its tether and had taken a short cut.

After Spring Hotel opened, we no longer stayed at the Sunny Caribbee. It was then that the owners cleared land around the hotel for factory-made houses shipped from the Guyana Timber Company. A lovely salt water pool and beach bar were built for the complex.

In the late 1980s a bad fire destroyed the main hotel building. After lying in ruins for a time, it was rebuilt in a grand manner. It has been operating ever since as the "Plantation House," but to those who remember, it will always be the "Sunny Caribbee."

WHISTLER

The Whistler was "the" boat in 1964 that linked Bequia to the rest of the world. Built in 1906, she looked a hundred years old. Today she lies rotting at the bottom of the Caribbean, but in the "beginning" she was our splendid transportation. She and her crew were unusually hard workers. Occasionally, just after pay day, there was a time when she was "not working." It was such a time that a group of us staying at the Sunny Caribbee decided to do an unheard of thing and "charter the Whistler."

What a great sight as we sailed out of Admiralty Harbor for Union Island where we would overnight. A rusted Coca-Cola cooler had been commandeered from a local bar and was well stocked with rum punch, gimlets, beer and an assortment of soft drinks. The hotel had provided hampers of food for the trip down. Tommy Providence, a congenial young giant, came along to keep us safe. It was a most pleasant sail with a short side trip for an over-the-side swim at Canuouan.

Rather than swim, Karl elected to venture out on the Sailfish that had been brought aboard at the last moment. Because she had been rigged improperly by the last user, Karl sat cross-legged on the board working on knots. Unbeknownst to him, however, the current was strong and swift, bearing him surely toward Venezuela. Many "halloos" from the rest of us brought no response, for the trade winds carried off our voices. It was, perhaps, twenty minutes later that he completed his work and looked up, ready to hoist the sail. Then he discovered the Whistler to be far in the distance. With a wind barely stronger than the current, he struggled to regain lost distance on the tiny boat. It was with a big kiss and a sigh of relief that I greeted him as he climbed aboard an hour or so later.

Since we'd been so concerned about Karl's departure, the swimming venture was aborted. So, as we neared our destination, we decided to stop off for a really good swim at the Tobago Keys…just a short sail from Union Island.

Being of a non-layering and all-for-comfort persuasion, Marilyn hadn't donned her swim suit beneath her outer clothes as had the rest of us. When the anchor was dropped at the Keys and we stripped of shorts and shirt, Marilyn had a bit of a problem. With the Whistler's cabin filled with crew members there was no private changing room. She turned to Charlie with the query, "Where can I put on my suit so no one will see?" In those early days the beautiful harbor at the Keys was almost empty of yachts. There were only two. Off the bow was a tiny boat. From it came a dog's bark as we could barely see a small dachshund racing around the deck. Astern and to port was a sleek black yacht. She had a larger crew. We could see white-jacketed figures walking along her deck. Charlie took a look around. "Well, there are just those two yachts and they're too far away to be a problem. Come on back. There's a space behind the wheelhouse and I'll stand guard while you're changing." That's just how the problem was solved. Marilyn leaned against the wheelhouse so as not to lose her balance as she changed into her swim clothes.

It was well worth the stop, we all decided as we snorkeled and played in the crystal clear waters.

Arriving at Union Island about five o'clock, we were greeted by an over-abundance of eager villagers in dinghies

"Taxi!"

ready to transport us ashore. That we did and crossed the
island by taxi (I use the word loosely) to the Queen Elizabeth
Hotel, where our party was booked overnight. You must real-
ize that this was 1964, a bare year after planes came to these
smaller Caribbean islands, so that tourists, especially white
tourists, were a rarity. The Queen Elizabeth Hotel was thus-
ly named because her Highness had stopped there for tea on
a Caribbean junket, and these were loyal subjects. It boasted
the only jukebox in the southern Caribbean.

After our party was settled in (we filled the hotel), it was
downstairs for a specially prepared dinner. As we'd
approached the hotel, I'd noticed a mountain of conch shells.
Now I learned where they'd come from. They were the end
result of our dinner menu. First, we enjoyed conch chowder.

Then came conch appetizers, followed by fried conch, conch fritters and conch salad. If they'd heard of conch ice-cream, I'm sure we'd have been served that, too. But we did have our own private open-air dining room. Well, almost private, since a very large white pig kept walking in and out through the open door to observe the visitors.

After a few rum punches, we all retired to our rooms. Karl and I were privileged to have the only one directly over the room with the jukebox. Everyone in the southern Caribbean must have plugged the juke box that night. I know that by 3:30 a.m., I'd learned every word of all twenty records, but, at least, I was still in my bed.

The next morning we found Karen curled up on a veranda sofa. About 2:00 a.m., she'd left their room, at the rear of the hotel and close by the generator house, to quiet some yowling cats. The door banged shut behind her and with the generator noise and George's snoring, she couldn't make herself heard and had spent the night on the lumpy sofa. We thought it was much funnier than Karen did.

We taxied back to the Whistler through a cheering throng of black-black school children, all of whom spoke beautiful Oxford English. School had been dismissed for the day so that they might greet us.

As our sunburned party sailed back into lovely Admiralty Bay, we vowed never again to leave the civilization of Bequia.

The next evening, as we lounged near the bar, sipping our cocktail-hour rum punches, four nattily-dressed men joined us and introduced themselves as officers of the Ring Anderson, which had sailed into Admiralty Harbor that afternoon. We introduced ourselves, speaking of our recent adventure on the Whistler. The captain of the Ring Anderson turned to Marilyn and chuckled as he said, "Oh, yes, we've seen you before. You're the one with the mole on her left hip." Poor Marilyn, she turned twelve different colors of red as he continued, "Oh yes, it was great entertainment for the whole group. We'd had our glasses trained on the Whistler to see who had introduced her into the charter fleet. When you went back of the wheelhouse we had a clear shot. Ah yes...believe me, young lady, there were quite a few comments."

These days, Marilyn probably changes behind closed doors.

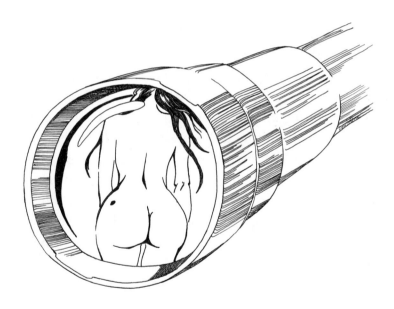

PLUM BELLY

Her name was "Plum Belly" and she sat on top of the water looking like a Caribbean child's coconut boat. Before that she was laid up on stilts on the golden sands of Port Elizabeth. Klaus Alverman, her young German builder and owner, a most innovative architect of Caribbean homes, was readying his jewel for a round-the-world adventure. She tugged at her hawser and lifted her bow at each wave. The Plum Belly was a miniature sloop, self designed and outfitted with minimal amenities for her bachelor owner.

Down the beach several hundred yards or so, around the corner past the Frangipani Hotel and the Crab Hole, George and Karen Cummings were at dinner in the company of their fellow adventurers vacationing at the Sunny Caribbee. They, however, were returning to Midwest snows. It was Friday and on the next day George, a trial attorney, had to depart Bequia in order to meet a Monday morning trial date in Iowa. It was imperative that he depart LIAT's St. Vincent flight to Barbados, connecting with another to the States. That meant a 6:30 a.m. departure aboard the Whistler for the nine mile crossing of the Bequia channel.

Karen was not a morning person. She had even sweet talked the maids into an eye-opener carafe of coffee in her room, an unheard of amenity on Bequia. So she, as usual, was complaining,

"George, we'll have to leave on that damned early morning boat and spend the whole day in St. Vincent. I just won't do it. We've got to charter."

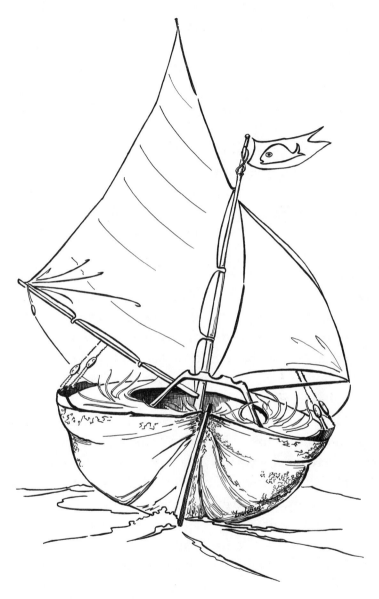

"Plum Belly"

This positive statement was accompanied by all the histrionics of a former college dramatic arts major and community theater thespian. George was no Casper Milquetoast, but there were times (nearly always) when he recognized the value of silence.

As Klaus lounged at the nearby hotel bar enjoying his third rum punch, he looked the shapely blonde up and down and made a spot decision.

"Mrs. Cummings, my boat the Plum Belly is here in the harbor. I'm about to take her solo on her maiden voyage, but I wouldn't mind a shakedown cruise with company. Could I offer the two of you a ride to the mainland tomorrow at your convenience?"

It could only have been a gift from heaven. Arrangement made for a post lunch departure left Karen time for a last morning in the sun. As the rest of us lunched in the open air dining room, we wished "safe passage" and promised to call as soon as we were back in Iowa. Sail set to the sky, the Plum Belly stood out of Admiralty Bay, met the Caribbean, rounded the headland north and disappeared.

There are two versions of what happened in the following eighteen hours. They bear little resemblance to each other. Perhaps Klaus's story should be given the greatest credence as all of us knew Karen would not be self-effacing.

The steady, dependable trade winds failed to comprehend the importance of George's stateside appointment and, being on Caribbean time, decided that after lunch would be a good time to stop working. They did just that; they quit blowing.

With the wind down and the Plum Belly in irons, to be helpful George went below deck to start the engine. After looking around without finding it, he called up to Klaus for its location. It was only then that George learned there WAS no engine — purist Klaus was planning to sail round the world nature's way — by wind power.

With the sail luffing, the Plum Belly and her three beleaguered passengers caught the southwest currents through the islands of the Grenadines and drifted rapidly into the ink of Caribbean waters.

Klaus had followed the cardinal rule of Caribbean sailors — "Never leave port without fresh water and rum" — except for the rum he substituted Scotch. By mid-afternoon when Karen was sunburned and grumpy, she made her first trip below deck. There she discovered both the Scotch and the water. Since she was most unhappy with the turn of events, she locked herself in the cabin and there disposed of both — first the Scotch and then, with evil intent, the water. She used it all in washing and rinsing her blonde tresses thoroughly to remove all trace of salt. Triumphantly, then she unlocked the cabin door, went up the ladder and announced to the two sunburned men what she had done. They didn't kill her — I'm sure they wanted to — but they just sat there squinting into the sun while drifting further and further south toward Venezuela.

Perhaps Neptune decided they had been punished long enough. Toward sunset the wind came up. By just after midnight, the Plum Belly had sailed up past Bequia with the hope of making a landfall at St. Vincent, not at the regular harbor, but at a rocky point far to the west. Still, thought George, there would be time for a shower at the Sugar Mill, where their overnight booking was being wasted, if they could get a fast taxi ride to the airport.

It was at this point that Klaus's endurance began to weaken. For hours he had been silently cursing his unfortunate proffer. Now, with luck, these people soon would be off his boat and away. He'd be damned, though, if he'd chance a hole in the hull from rocks along shore. It was better to break out the rubber dinghy he had lashed astern for emergencies. By God — this was an emergency.

Into the water astern went the dinghy and into the dinghy went the skipper with a harness over his chest and shoulders and rope around his waist. Klaus was strong and he pulled mightily on the oars. Meanwhile, George stood on deck with a lantern, peering hopefully into the darkness to search out some sign of land. Karen was stationed at the bow with orders to release the anchor as soon as the word was given. Klaus wanted to anchor bow out, safely away from the rocks. At intervals George hallooed to Klaus, inquiring as to the headway the lone man was making, rowing a rubber dinghy — pulling the sloop against wind and tide. Surprisingly, he was making progress. After some time, word was passed to George that Karen should drop the anchor.

Dropping the anchor was another first for Karen, a land-locked Midwesterner. She was naturally hesitant about bold moves and was letting out the chain gingerly. In the mean-time the boat was drifting closer and closer to the rocks so that George screamed,

"For Christ's sake, Karen, drop the anchor!"

Karen did not like someone to yell at her — not George — not anyone. Drop the anchor she did. Its weight and the long journey through the deep water gave it such momentum that when the anchor reached the end of the chain it didn't stop; it pulled out its bolt in the stem and, with a mighty splash, anchor chain and all disappeared through the hawsepipe into the black water.

There they were then, no anchor and the Americans still aboard. Within minutes, Karen and George were ordered

"...this was an emergency."

into the dinghy with all their luggage. Klaus, still at the oars, rowed to the rocky shoreline. There they were unceremoniously dumped into the deserted darkness and bid farewell — forever.

Leaving Karen to guard the luggage, George stumbled down a dirt, rock strewn road to reach a shack where there was resting, unbelievably, a dilapidated car. With George's persistent banging, a light appeared in the window, then a sleepy man opened the door. He proved to be a kindly off-duty policeman. Dressing quickly, he and George got into the car, returned for Karen, and off they putted for Kingstown and the Sugar Mill.

It was false dawn as George paid his benefactor and tried the door at the hotel. It was locked against intruders. Picking up some pebbles, George tossed them against a window of a room he knew to be occupied by friends. They awakened when the thrown pebbles shattered the glass. But at last, exhausted and filthy, they were in their own hotel room. After a quick shower, change of clothes and trip to the airport, they were on the right plane, at the right time, flying to the right place.

Oh, yes! when George entered the courtroom on Monday morning, he found the trial had been continued due to the illness of the judge. *C'est la vie!*

Manicoo

BITS AND PIECES
(Well, what really hoppen!)

THIRST

Julie's crew was brushing off a newly-sold tract of land just west of us. As the heat of the day increased, so did the men's thirst. Karl answered a halloo at the kitchen side of our octagonal open house to find a tall, skinny young man standing there.

"Mr. Fischer, would there be a thermos of ice I might have, please?"

Karl rummaged in the lower cupboard in search of the one thermos left us by a long series of petty thieves. He filled it with ice and handed it to the young man as he asked, "How about a little water in it?"

The young man smiled an engaging smile as he looked at Karl.

"Well, Mr. Fischer, would you have something else to make my eyes shine a little brighter?"

CATCHING MANICOO

Manicoo (possum to you) is a Bequia delicacy nonpareil. Shortly after our arrival on the island in the early 1960s, we witnessed the skill needed to snare the elusive creature. Burt (our car starter-pusher) was about eight at the time, a wiry towhead with sharp eyes and quick hands. When he whipped out his knife to cut a stick with one section of the "Y" longer than the other and sharpened the short portion to a wicked looking point, we held our breath and just watched. Burt shinnied up the tree where he'd spied the manicoo. Prodding deep into its hole, in short order, he withdrew the stick and the manicoo, which was hooked securely under the jawbone with the simple weapon. A sharp jerk and out it came, flying through the air and falling to the ground below. As it lay stunned from its fall, Burt also returned to the earth by a quick tree slide, and, after pulling some stout blades of a nearby wild grass, picked up the manicoo by the tail and whirled it over his head. Then, while it was still dizzy he tied its front feet behind its back with wild grass strands, and nonchalantly threw it over his shoulder (much as Huck Finn with a fishing pole), carrying it home where Gramma would prepare a succulent stew.

MAKING CHARCOAL

Poor Elmer. He was so worried that Spring would be deforested by the charcoal makers. Of course, cutting did need to be kept under control. Elmer would waken to discover another patch of bay leaf (wild cinnamon) had fallen prey to the cutlass. In a hand-dug pit, coconut husks arranged as a lining were lighted. When the hot coconut fire burned down, the bay leaf branches were added in neat piles and the whole covered with a thick layer of green banana leaves. This combination smoldered until the low heat had burned everything but the carbon in the wood, thereby reducing it to charcoal. After the process was finished, the pit uncovered and their residue cooled, pieces of charcoal were heaped into baskets, carried the mile back to the harbor on women's heads and used as fuel for coal pots in which island cooking was done.

HUSKING COCONUTS

There may be a twentieth-century process, but nature's way is still used on Bequia. Let us begin with the coconut palm. Immediately below the seventy-foot canopy grow the bunches of coconuts. When they are ripe, they fall. Then plantation ladies load them into reed baskets and carry them on their heads to a pile where the husker sits. Between his legs and relatively close to his body rests a hoe…its working edge filed sharp. Grasping the nut at each end, the husker forces it against the sharpened hoe as he pulls it toward him. The husk falls open, revealing the nut. The nut is passed to another man who holds it in his left hand as he strikes it with just the proper force at its center with a knife-sharp cutlass held in his right hand. The nut, now "busted" into halves, is tossed into another basket and carried to drying sheds. These sheds consist of a cement floor and shallow walls along which runs a rail. The halved nuts are placed on the cement floor…meat side up. When all the nuts have been placed so, the roof is slid shut and the tropical sun heat does its job. Because of the differing coefficient of expansion between the hull and the meat, the now copra-meat loosens from the hull. Copra is packed into burlap bags until there is a large enough shipment to be sent to the coconut oil factory in St. Vincent. Hulls are piled into heaps and carried to the mile away harbor town in baskets on the heads of women. There the husks are made into charcoal for use in local cooking.

SYDNEY MAC

We always knew, as did the rest of the island, that Sydney Mac was a rou'e. He was a pincher and a squeezer. When we first came to Bequia, in February of 1964, we thought Sydney was a well-preserved old man. Twenty-two years later we realized he'd been a dissipated young man. One January first, he wakened away from his own home. The New Year's Eve party had brought him to seek a bed on the beachside in an unoccupied gingerbread house. He reached for his false teeth on the bedside table. No teeth. Hearing raucous laughter, Sydney staggered to the front porch in time to see a group of people watching a dog running along the beach with a set of teeth not its own. Someone laughingly caught the dog and returned the teeth to their embarrassed owner. Happy New Year, Sydney!

BONANZA

In February of 1976, a worker was nailing wallaba shingles to the roof of Ann Blair's house, which was perched on a rocky headland of Industry Bay. He noticed heavy wave action between the reef and shore in an area that was normally calm. Descending to the bay, he took a closer look. The bay was alive with bonita. A large school had traveled in through the only narrow break in the reef and was frantically circling to find its way out. Having no other means, the roofer ran two miles to the harbor where he passed on his news. Soon all available vehicles, plus walkers carrying tubs, buckets and boxes, converged on Industry Beach. Seining nets overflowed with fish on the first swipe. Many bonita were jumping out on the sand where people captured their wriggling bodies and filled containers. Land Rovers returned to the harbor trip after trip...full to the top. Everything on the island was filled. Fish left over were boated to St. Vincent. The glut destroyed the fish market for months.

NO ROOM

Portly, prosaic Stewart had captured the heart of wispy Beatrice. On this, the first of many visits to Bequia, Stewart visited Daphne's Creations for a fitting on a custom-made pair of shorts. As he modeled them behind the seclusion of a curtain, Daphne's full throated voice carried to the shop full of buyers, "No room for de balls...no room for de balls!" The problem must have been remedied, for when Stewart wore his new shorts the next day, he was decently covered, but he was never able to live down Daphne's exclamation.

RESULTS

During the 1950s, there was a surplus of cats on Bequia. Then, for a dozen years, there were none; some disease had cleaned them off the island. Now the cat population was once more burgeoning. Those cats were fair game to Donovan, a part-time hotel bartender. One night during dinner the dining room resounded with horrendous yowling. We investigated in the kitchen and watched Donovan swinging a lasso round and round his head. At the end of the rope swung the cat, noose around its neck and yowling so it could be heard in Port Elizabeth, several miles away. It was a sure way to keep the cat out of the kitchen.

WISE

Bill and Yvonne knew more on their first day on Bequia than other whites with a decade of residence. As is usual with know-it-alls, it was fruitless to warn them of dire results. So they chartered a fishing boat and were on the sea during the sun's beating down hours. By dinner, Bill's feet were swollen to the size of small red boats or bloated dead fish. It was then he vowed to drink the bar dry of gin. Bill's next trip into the sunshine was when they left the island. True to his vow, he had consumed the hotel's entire stock of gin. A trip to the mainland was necessary to replenish the liquor cabinet for other guests.

RUM

Caribbean air and the first day of holidays often make guests a little "nutty." Between the three o'clock arrival of the packet boat and five o'clock, George had consumed more than an adequate number of strong rum punches. No one stopped his staggering steps to the pool when he decided a dip might clear his head. Swan dive — almost! Swan song — almost! Into the shallow end of the pool he walrused...breaking his nose as he banged into the three-feet-deep bottom. Poor George! He survived, but wondered whether to blame his pounding headache on rum or diving.

and more rum

Another first day of rum brought a late dinner hour to a middle-aged hotel guest. His buxom, blonde German wife (much younger) had been matching him drink for drink. At dinner, Jim was seated on his one side and I on the other. Suddenly, in the midst of conversation, down went his head into the soup, with a second stage of slow crumpling as he slid off the chair and lay prone on the stone floor. Heart attack? Death? Ah no, narcolepsy. Furthermore, it was such a common occurrence that his wife didn't pause between bites or sentences.

JUMBIE DANCE

"Jumbie Dance" seemed a natural for the name of the hotel honeymoon cottage. To you Northerners, let me explain that jumbies are like zombies, those departed bodies who return at the time of the full moon. They dance in a closed circle, so the grassless ring close by our building must be the result of jumbie frolics. But, alas, the name was not to be. We were told that such sacrilege would offend the spirits and, in addition, no locals would set foot in the place to clean or repair if it had such a name. So it became the prosaic "Little Fort" as legend lost a round to practicality.

LAST RITES

Funerals are an important event on Bequia. In fact, loss of life seems to take a back seat to the funeral itself. For starters, let me tell you that, for twenty-five-cents a month, many Bequians subscribe to a Benevolent Association. Benefits of such membership are much desired. It assures the deceased of mourners, wailers, and a funeral procession from home to church to cemetery, guided by a leader in a black stovepipe hat and a long black frockcoat. He is followed by the casket, family and members of the Benevolent Society, be they friend or foe. This is an impressive sendoff.

more last rites

Of necessity, funerals are almost instantaneous on Bequia, due to the absence of embalming. One February morning, Teresa, a maid at our hotel, boarded the 6:30 a.m. Whistler for a marketing trip to St. Vincent. Teresa lived with her grandmother, who saw her off at the boat. On Teresa's return at 3:30 p.m., she was stunned to learn that during her nine-hour absence from Bequia, her grandmother had sickened; her grandmother had died; her grandmother's funeral had taken place; her grandmother had been buried and now lay in the graveyard behind the church. That's fast and final.

MAY-DAY

Karl was guarding the emergency channel of our marine radio when a MAY-DAY call came over, "MAY-DAY! MAY-DAY! We are a sixty-five-foot centerboard ketch. We have hit a reef and are taking on water. Our location is the windward shore of Bequia."

"MAY-DAY!"

Wow! that was our location. We looked through glasses and, sure enough, there she was, just outside Industry Reef. Another call. "MAY-DAY! MAY-DAY! We cannot make it to harbor. We think we can put into the next bay."

Karl jumped. "The next bay. That's Spring Bay. That ketch can't come into Spring Bay. The break in the reef isn't deep or wide enough."

Oh?

Wrong!

In through the reef she came, continuing till she was stuck tight on the sand of our shallow bay.

By then all sorts of thing started popping. Pumps and vehicles came from the harbor. The grandstand, normally our sea wall, was filled with observers offering a variety of suggestions. Finally, chugging along at full speed, a towboat arrived. With the rescue vessel standing by outside the reef, she set off a small boat carrying a light line which was passed to the foundering ketch. This was used to bring in an inch-and a-half nylon line. A harness was then designed to fit around the deckhouse of the stricken yacht and the tug started steaming seaward. The ketch stayed well stuck as the line stretched thinner and thinner to a half inch.

Karl remarked to no one in particular, "My God, that line will break and decapitate everybody on deck."

But good fortune ruled the day, as with a mighty whump, she came loose and, stern first, shot over the reef and past the tug. After she lost momentum they reset the lines. At last sight, she rounded the headland floating placidly behind her rescuer.

INSURANCE

Despite touting a relationship with Lloyds of London, St. Vincent insurance companies in the 60s and 70s left a great deal to be desired. Herb, our first manager, took out a policy which supposedly covered us against fire and wind, with added payments for additional coverage. It was only when we tried to collect on damage resulting from a "grudge" fire set in the banana shed that the fine print surfaced. In truth the policy read, "All buildings on Spring Estate are covered by this policy except those used for commercial purposes." Since we were a functioning hotel, that policy conveniently excluded all buildings on Spring Estate. The claim was denied. Karl threatened to sue for malfeasance, and they changed their minds.

We were one of the first to request coverage for our hotel and plantation workers shortly after the Workmen's Compensation Act was passed in the islands. Our manager, Mort, and the insurance agents were about equally informed. Spring Hotel's worker's compensation insurance premiums were based on a percentage of the hotel's payroll. One day, Vincent Glynn, while using a power mower in cutting grass, reached down to remove a rock from under the mower and in the process also removed his thumb. This time we learned our insurance covered "all employees with the exception of the following...." The exclusion listed, by name, every single employee on the plantation. When we asked just what we were paying for, the company representative replied, "Good question." Claim denied. Karl appealed on the grounds of malfeasance. Immediate reversal.

A third go-round with the insurance company occurred

when managers Sam and Ellen bought a new Land Rover for Spring Hotel without telling us about it. They put the title in their name and chose not to carry collision and upset insurance because the premium was so high for a rag-top. Several weeks later, their successor, Sue Hanson, ran the new Rover into a ditch —totaling it. She had not yet been added to the payroll as she had not received her first pay check. A claim was filed for both auto and Sue's injuries. Claims denied. No appeal. Our managers weren't very good business people.

BAKER...NONPAREIL

Margaret, above all, was considerate. For her planned surprise of Valentine Day cookies, she hand carried precious chocolate chips to Bequia — 2,750 air miles. Even after she tripped over a roving coconut and broke her ankle (so that it was encased in plaster), she carried on. All other cookie necessities, she bought locally in the traditional see-through plastic bag, self-knotted at the top. She mixed a triple batch of cookies and decided to have one taste before popping them into the oven. Actually, one- and a-half cups of sugar is preferable to one- and a-half cups of salt when baking gift cookies! Try, try again!

CHRISTMAS TRAGEDIES

In the mid-70s we almost hated to have the Christmas season approach. Tragedies. The first was the Christmas boat from Cannouan to St. Vincent bringing workers up the Grenadine chain for holidays with their families. She was heavily overloaded, of course, since everyone feared another

"Barrels floated in on the tide..."

boat wouldn't come in time to reach home. Life jackets were locked away to keep thieves from stealing them. A passenger shouted, "Whale!" Everyone rushed to one side of the boat, which turned turtle from the suddenly added weight. Loss of life was high.

The following year, in mid-December, we read the news in the "Vincentian," that a cargo ship had foundered in the channel between St. Lucia and St. Vincent. Barrels floated in on the tide, beaching near a village. They were filled with alcohol, enough for a big party. However, it turned out to be wood alcohol. Many samplers died and others were blinded...a sad finale to a celebration.

Clive Frank was a young man destined to be of influence in the Grenadines. Educated by the local Anglican schools and the London School of Journalism, Clive was an intelligent, thinking man of vision. In a third year of Christmas tragedies, Clive and his pilot were making a landing approach at Union Island. Something malfunctioned. We learned of the loss only when pieces of wreckage floated ashore from their sea grave.

HUMMERS

One of the three varieties of hummingbirds visiting our home in Bequia, as on other islands in the Lesser Antilles, is the "Crested Antillean." It is strong, sooty, brazen and quick as a wink. It flashes in and out of our bougainvilleas on a regular basis, and we usually get but a fast glimpse as its emerald green iridescence gleams in the sunlight. It harvests nectar from our thousands of hibiscus, and white cedar blossoms as well, with such speed it is virtually invisible.

Once we found a nest, tea strainer like, with a tiny entrance in one side of the bottom. The eggs were the size of little jelly beans.

Yesterday we had a new experience with the little creature. As Karl crouched low in some Ixoras, running the hose on the thirsty plants next to our stone porch, a tiny black hummer darted straight to the heart of a bush. Karl stared, rigid, as a scant foot from his face, the hummer perched on the edge of a scooped out leaf holding a miniature bath and then fluttered happily there. When all of the water was gone he rocketed off, leaving Karl unnerved.

Karl called to describe the episode to me, and, while he was pointing out the place of the performance, it was repeated for the two of us. So much for the small bird shows!

SHORTAGES

In the 1970s and 80s, there was always a shortage of something on Bequia, our small island of little consequence to the outside traders. Unless there was a drought, we could depend on pigeon peas, garden produce, flour and salt. One year rice, normally shipped from Trinidad in one-hundred-pound burlap bags, failed to reach the island. A staple of the Bequia diet had been eliminated. Another year it was sugar (in the land of sugar cane) that Barbados shipped elsewhere. Then, the lack was onions. That year, two or three in a plastic bag were treated as gold. Yearly, at Christmas and Easter when baking was heaviest, eggs were at a premium. To this day in the mid-90s, when there are eggs for sale in Bequia markets, they soon disappear into someone's basket for future needs. Unrefrigerated eggs never seem to rot.

PAN

What can you do with a steel drum?
Fill it with oil
                    or
Play it........
    Cut it.......
            Heat it...........
                    Pound it.........
Fill it to the brim with Bequia music...........
Let it run over 'till it floods the hills and valleys........
Calypso beat..........thumping feet...........
Find happiness at the end of the steel band rainbow
On an enchanted island.

March 12, 1966

SOUNDS

A quatro and a flute
And rhythm.............
Calypso beat, calypso feet
And rhythm.............

1967

MEMENTOS

In the 1960s there was no such thing as airport "security." One checked baggage, was assigned a seat and boarded the aircraft. But with the advent of high-jacking and terrorists all that changed. Everyone was very nervous about bombs on planes and in airports, and we'd been warned that light banter on the subject of firearms led only to arrest by security police.

Karl and Ray were returning to Iowa from Bequia…hand carrying two of the Portuguese glass fishing balls that had floated to Bequia's shore from Portugal. Covered with rotten net they had broken away from the rest of the nets. It was Ray's turn to carry them as the two men made their way down the busy concourse of J.F.K. airport. Ray decided an over-the-shoulder carry would be much superior to a normal suitcase carry. With a mighty heave, he slung the first ball above his head. You've guessed it, of course. The rotted netting securing the ball broke again. This time it resulted in a trajectory about forty feet over the tiled floor, imploding with a loud "BOOM" as it landed. There was anxiety everywhere as passengers and police rushed to-and-fro around a suspected bombing.

The two Iowans kept on walking and didn't look back. Not until they were in the air on the way to Chicago did they heave a big sigh of relief.

TO RAY, RE THE "FORTRESS"
An architect's folly

Oh carry me not
To the Fortress high
Where the curtains flap
And the wind howls free
And when I die
Please don't bury me
'Neath the Bequia sky
By a coconut tree.

For the two-ton doors
Are not raised by man
With an aching back
Labor's one excuse.
If you leave them shut,
Then its night all day
With the banshee wind
All night in your ears.

If they open stay,
Myriad stars to view,
Then the driving rains
Thunder in by two.
So your clothes get wet
And the mattress too.
But the doors won't shut
So you lie and stew
Till the dawn comes up
And the workmen too.

And the potty chair
Is a throne of gold
Where the subjects all
Do their homage pay
For the water pipe
And the garbage can
And the chipping stone
And the new clothesline
There they all converge
By the bathroom screen.
So when'er I sit
Still do others stare.

And the more I'm here
Where the curtains flap
Where the barn door shakes
With no sleep for me
Then the more I long
For a solid wall
And a rain-free bed
On the "Isle Bequia."

But until you live
In the "Fortress" high
You can't understand
Of what I do prate
So please.......get well........
Change this "Mickey Mouse,"
Lest my woman's heart
Turn from love to hate.

March 11, 1967

THE SCOTCH MCINTOSHES

We had already suffered through business dealings for Spring with Cecil, the eldest McIntosh. Next was Sydney, the middle brother, who kept our $5,000 down payment to buy Industry after our Aliens' License had been denied. Ignoring a signed contract with us, Sydney made another with Fred Wagner — for a better price — then saw to it that our first-made application to hold land at Industry was denied by the ministers. Our final introduction to the brothers McIntosh was to Howard, or "Buntie" as he was known locally. We had been warned to stay away from Buntie. Rumor had it that he had left the island under a cloud of some kind. However, he still owned his share of the family land, Raintree Estate. If you wanted to own any part of that estate, you were required to deal with Buntie.

Karl received a letter from Buntie, who was at his home in Trinidad. At the time we had never met him. He wondered if we had any interest in any part of Raintree. If so, he said he would like to meet us in Trinidad. Karl responded by telling him we might be interested in a little piece on the west side of the main road through his estate that was adjacent to Spring. We had already constructed a road in the area that would service such a piece. We, in turn, got another letter from Buntie advising that, indeed, he would consider such a sale, asking us to meet him in Trinidad. Karl and I made arrangements to go to Trinidad to see him, as requested, and then notified Buntie of our time of arrival.

Upon arrival in Trinidad, we taxied to Howard's home.

Karl returned shortly to state Howard had asked to be our dinner guest at the Hilton. We could then discuss the price he wanted for Raintree and the other terms of sale. Agreed. He told Karl what he wanted and of the rather simplistic terms of sale. Karl accepted them without equivocation and then burned the midnight oil writing the contract. Next day he presented it to Howard, who, with a taxi driver as witness, signed the document. We then flew back to St. Vincent and delivered the contract to our attorney. He prepared the necessary application for an Aliens' License that was duly approved by the ministers several months later. Karl also employed a Vincentian surveyor to plot the property and get approvals from the Office of Lands and Surveys. More money down the drain!

Between the signing of our contract with Buntie and the time our Aliens' License was approved, Buntie called us twice and asked for favors. First, he wanted a mangle for his wife. We got in touch with Sears of Canada and had the company send the desired item by fast freight. Then he called to ask us to send him an automatic washing machine. It was done. Same way.

Our lawyer called to tell us he had prepared the deed from Buntie. Karl called the latter to tell him we would be flying to Trinidad on a particular date for the sole purpose of completing our contract with him.

Once more we flew to Trinidad and again went to Howard's house by taxi. Howard refused to see us, saying he would come to the hotel. There, in our room, he refused to sign the deed or accept our check, saying, "You knew the value of my property and I didn't." He went on to say that we had "overreached" him.

I cowered behind the closed bathroom door listening to

my ordinarily placid husband deliver a diatribe of the choicest navy terms for a chiseler of Howard's ilk. Before final slamming of the door, Karl described in detail the stone coffin which would contain Howard's body and be sunk at sea if he EVER were to appear on Spring Estate in Bequia.

Today, all three are dead. At night one light flickers in Industry. Raintree lies across the bay from us — dark and windswept — and undeveloped.

Readers might be interested in knowing we never had our down payment returned, nor were we ever reimbursed for the funds advanced on the mangle and washing machine.

"Today we had guests for breakfast...
a pair of yellow banana quits..."

YELLOW-BIRD TALES

Looking across the endless blue water from an open-air dining room is the best possible way to start the day. In earlier times, when we thought electricity was a necessity, we had the house wired and carried an exotic ceramic lamp from the States. But the generator had been in disrepair for years, and the filigreed lamp served only a decorative purpose. That is, until this morning. Today we had guests for breakfast…a pair of yellow banana quits who were in search of a safe place to build their springtime love nest. They carried on a spirited conversation. Finally, they flew away in search of building materials. In and out of the lamp they fluttered with their treasures until a goodly number of grasses and twigs rested inside the bottomless cylinder. But their work was to no avail, for each sprig added, two fell out the bottom. After an hour, they abandoned the project, only to reappear next morning to try again with renewed vigor. Day after day they tried to build that nest, and day after day twigs fell out the bottom of the lamp. Then one morning, Karl and I found ourselves alone at breakfast. There was a new yellow-bird nest in the pink hibiscus bush at the side of the porch.

The yellow birds approved of our house and made it their own. One morning I returned to our bedroom bower for something. As I approached the house, I heard a wild chittering, so, walking quietly, I peeked into the bathroom. Perching on a candle chimney and facing the mirror, a tiny "quit" was carrying on a spirited conversation with its mirrored image. After several minutes, out the door she flew. She must have been narcissistic, however, as I caught her several times after that, perching on a glass or soap dish, peering into the mirror and chittering to herself.

Sexism is obvious in the yellow-bird community. We had hung a coconut husk feeder filled with local brown sugar, so there was a constant coming and going through daylight hours for a snack. We learned early on that theirs was a male dominated society. The larger male flew in first for a feeding. Only later, when he had finished, did the smaller and drab female make her appearance. And, if by chance, he flew by and noticed her enjoying herself, a chase followed. Bad bird!

The daily bath became a ritual. I set out a margarine tub half filled with fresh water each morning. After their sugar breakfast, our yellow birds would flit down for a drink from the edge, then hop in, splash for ten seconds or so, and fly off. They sometimes seemed to be waiting in line for their turn at the bathing tub. Since we were breakfasting less than ten feet away, their bathing ritual provided entertainment.

Our sugar birds may not have understood Spanish, but they firmly believed that "Su casa es mi casa." However, they had never watched me cook, so I was startled to see one perched on the top of the kitchen door as I kneaded bread dough. I said good morning and continued my labor. With a great twittering, he flew down to settle on a bowl almost at my elbow...then departed through the door. A minute or so later, he returned to pursue the same actions. I knew he wanted something from me — that was obvious — but what was it? And then I knew. His coconut bowl was empty. I filled the coconut husk with sugar. Mission accomplished, my friend returned to his snack bar and I returned to my bread dough. Over the following years, I answered so many of these summonses that Karl calls me the "bird lady."

FLAGS

Ginnie and Al Zavelle, former American Bequians, drove yesterday from Sarasota to spend the day with us at Naples. They told one of their favorite island stories. In the 1970s Bequia was not puritanical. Neither was it Bohemian. When guests from a French yacht ventured to Spring Beach for topless bathing, the binoculars came out.

Keith Elwick's home, overlooking the beach at Spring, proved a vantage point for his observations. A former Zavelle guest had left behind a bikini with a sizable bra-top. Invited to an Elwick cocktail party, Ginnie surreptitiously added the bra to Keith's homemade flagpole, already sporting the Bequia flag, the Stars and Stripes, and the flag of Iowa. Everyone chuckled until, several days later, Keith noticed, and it was removed.

MAMA

Mama padded into our lives in January of 1988. She was a calico. At first we were misled into thinking she was a Manx, as her tail was bobbed. After examination, though, we could see someone had cut off her tail when she was a kitten, or she'd caught it somewhere, or she was naturally deformed. Our gardener called her "Stubby," but she was too delicate for that. And she would be a mama soon.

Even in her half-starved condition, she drank her cream politely. Plain bread would do, but piecing it with sardines was for a queen, thank you. Mama never begged for food but sat on her haunches before us, licking her chops in anticipation. Later she would thank us for thinking of her — rubbing gently against our legs or nuzzling our feet till we responded by scratching her ears or stroking her snowy fur.

By February it had been mutually agreed — we were hers and she was ours.

As birthing time neared, Mama craved added security, clumsily climbing into our laps for many of her cat naps. So it was not unexpected when she sat at our feet one evening as we read in adjoining chairs. Soft amber eyes pleaded as she added a tentative and unusual meow. I lifted her ungainly body to my lap, patted and settled her down, but her complaints continued as she moved awkwardly back and forth between our chairs.

Bedtime came and Mama followed us up the stone steps to our bedroom house. As the night time darkened, she jumped on the bed and snuggled between us, still crying piteously. I brushed her down or set her on the floor from time to time, but each time she discreetly reestablished herself on the bed.

"Pat, come see what's in our bed...."

By first light my patience was at an end.

"I've had it! That darned cat! I haven't slept all night! I'm going down to the main house and sleep in the guest bedroom!"

Karl acknowledged my departure sleepily as he continued to stroke the wailing cat, secluding her under the coverlet to mute the sound. He dozed on. Suddenly, he became aware that the intensity of the MEOWS had decreased about ten decibels and was then a series of very tiny noises. Sitting straight up in bed, he lifted the coverlet. The source of the noise was obvious…three wet kittens lying beside Mama, squeaking their little heads off.

Karl covered the distance between our two bedrooms in six leaps. "Pat, come see what's in our bed. Our Valentine's Day kittens have arrived!"

We left for the States two weeks later. The kittens still hadn't opened their eyes. We bought all of the cat food and sardines on the island and left instructions with our gardener to feed the family. But we regretted adopting and then abandoning our gentle Mama and feared for the worst without our help in feeding the family.

As I write this in February of 1990, Mama is up in our bedroom house, hidden behind two hammocks leaning in the corner of the closet. For each of the past several years she has settled for a padded box rather than our bed as her birthing room — although each year she tries for the bed. Mama growls when they make a noise, but she knows we know where she moved them after birth. An earlier offspring, "Fraidy-Cat," has joined our family. But in the past three years, we've never seen another of Mama's kittens with its eyes open; even though Mama is waiting for us each year when we return to our Bequia home.

and more cats

Mama had delivered her third batch of kittens in our bedroom closet three weeks before. We were also feeding "Fraidy" — a scaredy cat who needed a cat psychiatrist. In addition, "Pig" walked in regularly with a big yellow Tom to steal everything it could find. I had done everything I could to discourage the two from their visits to our house, but Pig, especially, was persistent.

This particular morning Karl had brought a couple to call. They had purchased a lot below us. As usual, we showed them the view from our bedroom house and told the "four-poster" story. Then we returned to our main house for a walk-through. Karl was in the bathroom discussing our Italian tile with George. I had explained my unique linen storage under the bed and pulled out a drawer to show the arrangement. Karl said I screamed so loud he thought I was having a heart attack. No, that wasn't it. Resting on a pile of bath towels were four brand new kittens. No parenting cat was in residence, but Pig had rightfully figured us as a soft touch for nourishing meals. No more brooms for this year — only milk and food for their bottomless bellies in this marvelous haven for unwed mothers.

THE WHALE

What a day for a picnic. What an unusual reason for a picnic. What a first for our early island days.

The whalers of Paget Farm on Bequia have been here now for generations. Formerly from New England, we are told they settled on this lovely island for two reasons: first, Bequia is on the route of the annual migration of whales; second, they wanted to escape the frigid waters of the North Atlantic. The change was one of latitude. They took whales around Bequia as their great grandfathers did up north. There is no widespread slaughter of whales here.

Rarely more than several times a year, a message is flashed, by mirror from the summit of Monkey Hill, to signal the crews of the little double-ended sailboats used for whaling. The boats are launched for their exciting hunt. When found and then harpooned by hand, the whale runs, boat following, until it floats dead. After those dangerous steps the whale is towed to a nearby island for processing. There the blubber is removed and the whale butchered.

On our picnic day, a whale had been taken and towed to Petit Nevis where there were processing facilities. Hearing about the whalers' good luck, Ellen, our manager at Spring Hotel in 1969, gathered supplies for a breakfast picnic. We piled into our Rover, chartered a sailboat from Isola's brother, Kennedy Frederick, and were off for Petit Nevis. So was every other available rowboat, motorboat and sailboat.

After sailing for an hour we rounded Moonhole with the rest of the regatta, reached a snug harbor at our destination

"Inside the carcass stood two men in hip boots."

and were set off into the boat's dinghy.

Barb and Ruth were among the party. We'd hardly stepped into our transportation ashore when Barb spied a motionless shark on the sand floor of our little bay. As she'd always wanted a shark-tooth necklace, she requested Kennedy to perform some quick dental work on the shark.

Obliging Barb, Kennedy slipped overboard and, knife flashing, seized the "dead" shark by the snout. Miracle of miracles! the shark was resurrected from the dead and flexed its body violently. Kennedy made a mighty surge to the gunwale of our boat...reaching safety about the same time as his bubbles. No shark teeth that day.

Safely ashore, we all climbed to a high overlook for a breakfast picnic. Our menu consisted of tinned sardines, beer, peanut butter sandwiches, rum cake, and pickles. Other picnics were underway all around us, little fires everywhere. Karl was the only one who seemed to be bothered by the pervasive odor of the matters at hand.

After breakfast we wound our way back down the hill where the whale was being butchered. What an assembly line! What cooperation! The whale was winched up gradually as each section was worked. Inside the carcass stood two men in hip boots. They cut the blubber into chunks several feet square and about a half a foot thick. These were tossed ashore and hauled to the hill. There the chunks were hacked into smaller pieces and thrown into huge vats to be boiled into oil. We were told the oil would go to England.

After the blubber had been removed, the red meat was exposed. It, too, was cut by the inside men, thrown ashore and hauled for processing by ladies, wives or relatives of the whalers. They worked under a tarpaulin to shade the fresh meat. An assembly line further cut the meat, deciding which should be used fresh, corned or cooked to preserve it.

To us, the most fascinating of the whole affair were the blubber cutters — at break they laid aside their cutlasses, sat down in a section that had been cut out and drank Pepsi. Karl gagged; it brought back experiences with cod liver oil.

By early afternoon, the whale processing had been completed. Tired families returned home with their bonanzas. The whale carcass, now stinking under a burning sun, was pushed back into the sea with long poles. Hundreds of sharks churned the blue Caribbean into a sea of red.

We sailed back to Bequia to the fragrance of frangipani, a welcome change.

MERRY-GO-ROUND
SARA SINDEBAND

Betty and Sindy found and purchased a lovely burro. The plan was to throw saddlebags over her back and use her to carry supplies home from the harbor. In those days transportation from Port Elizabeth to Spring Estate was minimal. Then came taxis and cars. "Sara" Sindeband was destined to spend her days tied to a coconut tree to graze on the lush pasture grass of our lowlands.

One lazy afternoon, Karl chugged down the hill on his mini-Honda to gather grapefruit from our orchard. He had to cross a cow yard that was grassed, with coconut trees growing every fifty feet or so. Sara and several cows were tethered to different trees and grazing there. Karl didn't want to pass near the cows and slip in their pies. Sara stood between Karl and his route to the grove.

Because he knew Sara would be frightened by the cycle, he gingerly drove around her tree, giving her what he thought was a wide berth. As he pulled abreast of Sara, she was about seventy-five feet from him. He frightened her, nonetheless, and she started to run.

For the first time Karl noticed Sara was not tied to the tree she was near. Instead she was tethered to a tree by a very long rope about four feet over the ground on the other side of his cycle. As Sara strained on her tether and it became taut, the rope was raised three feet or so over the ground.

As luck would have it, at that moment, the rope was right

"Sara"

under Karl's cycle. The front wheel was raised off the ground, caught on the rope. As Sara started to run around her tree, Karl's merry-go-round began. Round and round they circled, ever closer to the tree, then Sara balked and set her feet. Karl sailed through the air and landed on the ground where he lay bruised and battered. Eventually he limped up the hill to home and liniment.

MORNING GLORY TREE

There is a fairy tree overhanging the deck of our eyrie home. Botanically, it is named a tabebuia, locally, a white cedar, personally, a morning glory tree. In January, leaves begin to dry and fall, so the yard looks like autumn in Iowa. Amos spends many hours raking, hauling and burning. In February, after a few good showers, new leaves and flower buds appear to herald Bequia's spring blooming. One morning we awaken to a glorious display of light pink or white blossoms covering the tree. During the daylight hours, these petunia-like flowers parachute earthward so that by dusk our floor is a carpet. At the base of each blossom is a tiny slit, evidence of a visiting hummingbird or banana quit which has sipped its nectar. By nightfall, blossoms are an ugly brown. But the next dawn, fresh buds have opened and our morning glory tree is once more bedecked in beauty.

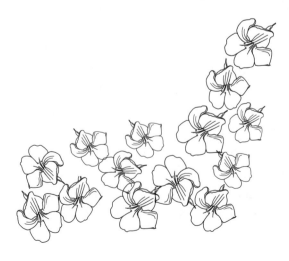

WHITHER THOU GOEST....

Anyone traveling with the O'Briens has known adventure. So it was with eyes open to the possibilities and probabilities that we agreed to deviate from the usual flight plan to Bequia and follow Pat O.B., our Pied Piper. Part of the intrigue is that only the leader knows the plan. The first instruction was to meet at Gate 4, Miami International Airport, to board Air Martinique's afternoon flight to that island. We also knew we were to overnight at some designated hotel in Martinique. The next day we were to board some type of seagoing vessel that would take us directly to Bequia, thereby avoiding St. Vincent packet boats. A total of eight would make up the party.

Karl and I arrived in Miami by car from Naples, purchased tickets, checked in and proceeded to the gate. When boarding was announced, we realized we were the only members of the party present. Nettie and Pete Snyder were flying in from California. No one in the boarding area seemed the right age to be the Snyders. Pat and Jim were obviously not there. That left Chris and Andy Loetscher. Chris, in her final year of the Iowa Physicians' Assistant program, was to receive credit from "in service" work at the Bequia Infirmary. Andy had one year remaining in dentistry and would be doing a month's internship with Dr. O'Brien. The two of them had left Iowa earlier and driven O'Brien's car to Miami...if they had arrived.

Ten minutes after we'd boarded and were cozily settled into our seats, a likely looking couple appeared, obviously looking for someone. Karl spied a service academy ring. We introduced ourselves. Fifty percent of the party then was present and accounted for. Another fifteen minutes brought an announcement from the flight deck. "Due to a delay in a connecting flight, we will be departing immediately after the arrival of eight expected passengers." There was no doubt as to the identity of two of those expected passengers. Hubbub at the door proved us right — O'Briens and their luggage, as well as Chris and Andy, who had been waiting forlornly in the boarding area for their tickets carried by the O'Briens.

So we were off. After a sunset flight, we landed in Martinique and informed the hotel of our arrival. "Who? No bookings for eight O'Briens." No confirmation money had arrived — no room in the inn. French efficiency at the Tourist Board located three rooms at one hotel, with a single at another. Within half an hour, Karl and I were snuggled under our sheets. Our window opened onto the park, with its murmur of conversation and taxis, peeping tree frogs and a balmy Caribbean breeze fluttering the curtains.

Early morning found us in the dining room breakfasting on fresh orange and soursop juice, freshly sliced pineapple, strong coffee, and croissants with jelly. Pete wandered in, followed shortly by a breathless Pat with word that there was a strike, and, therefore, no boats. "But if we leave now for the airport, we might catch the 9:00 a.m. flight to St. Vincent."

HAH! We were there, but the flight was full. So, while Andy and I sat on the pooled luggage, Chris wandered off to buy postcards. The rest of our party marched to other airlines to make alternate plans...a charter perhaps. No, but three hours later, a considerate Air Mustique manager escorted us to our gate with word that the flight to Union Island would divert to allow eight passengers to disembark at St. Vincent.

Suddenly we were landing...through customs and whisked into a taxi with piles of luggage tied on. We could smell the familiar "Sunshine Bakery" and the lovely aroma of the ilang-ilang tree by the airport and knew we were almost home.

But life is never easy, nor is the Bequia passage. We learned that the Friendship Rose had departed, but the Roll-On would leave at three, or four, or five, depending on whenever the water tanks had been filled and the twenty gasoline drums trundled aboard. That left time for a surprise reunion with Ann Joshua and a leisurely lunch at the Cobblestone, shopping at Greaves Supermarket, and the interminable wait for the hum of diesels and casting off of lines.

The channel was fairly calm. At the moment of the green flash, had there been one, we pulled into the harbor at Port Elizabeth. There was Julie with the same dancing eyes and wide smile, ready to lead us across the block to "Julie's Guest House." Isola came out then and, even after more than twenty years of friendship, our hugs were shy. But what a surprise! Waiting since two o'clock, dressed in their "program" red shirts and white blouses, was the girls' chorus. They sang a welcome song with sweet eight- to fourteen-year-old voices. Then the tall girl on the end stepped forward with a bouquet for me, a kiss and hug. It couldn't be Sarah, our thirteen-year-old goddaughter, lissome and lovely and so grown up. Another song, Sarah again to Karl, with a kiss and a gift for him. More celebration — champagne for the whole party, dinner at Isola's, into the car with Philmore and up the winding hill road to our eyrie...January, 1985...return to paradise.

"...the tall girl on the end stepped forward with a bouquet for me, a kiss and hug. It couldn't be Sarah, our thirteen-year-old goddaughter, lissome and lovely and so grown up."

10.42

Mrs. N. Taylor is our favorite baker. In the early morning hours, she rises to knead and mold the white and whole wheat bread that emerges warm and fragrant from her oven in time for breakfast sales. Mrs. Taylor is also the owner of a well stocked market and adjoining bar and restaurant. We frequently telephone to have bread put back for us till we coordinate errands for one trip to the harbor. One morning Karl entered the open-air door to find a young man at the cash register.

"I've come to collect the bread Mrs. Taylor saved for us today. How much do I owe you?"

"10.42," was the soft reply.

"I beg your pardon?"

"10.42."

Karl searched his pockets for change to add to his two $5.00 bills. "Just a minute. I'll have to get some change from my wife."

"Pat, I need 42 cents. Do you have it?"

I did indeed and the money was passed through the car window.

On Karl's return to the store, he lay down the 42 cents and two $5.00 bills, whereupon the young man shoved back the change to Karl who once again pushed it toward him. It was at that point the young man spoke slowly and distinctly.

"Ten - for - de - two."

After thirty-five years on Bequia, wouldn't you think we could understand plain English?

PART III

PERSONALITIES

GRAY

Gray clouds scudding,
A gray squall sheeting across the water,
Coming closer till my world is enveloped in a gray mist.
When the squall passes gray islands come into view.
Gray sails and sailboats are a silhouette on the gray sea
As white tipped waves break on gray rocks.
But see — a shaft of silver!
And another —
Sun breaking the gray clouds
With a promise.....

January 21, 1990

MANAGERS

Then there were the hotel managers. Ah yes!…the managers. With one exception, they were all good people capable in their own areas and brought to us by a dream not unlike our own — "paradise found." Herb, our first manager, really cared for the entire estate. During his brief tenure, he hid in his packing box and almost never came out till it was time to return to the Midwest. Brian replaced him. Brian was a friend of Ray Crites, one of our architects who insisted that Brian wouldn't charge us except for board and room. The first hint that this was not strictly true was when we arrived two weeks before the hotel's grand opening to see a tri-level elevator shaft reaching toward the sky from a cliff above the hotel. Ray casually commented that this was the new home we'd built for Brian in lieu of salary. Bequia was not an end-all for Brian. He was a bachelor accustomed to silver and bone china in the subdued surroundings of his mother's home, but he needed a rest. The year-long work permit he was granted made possible a sabbatical from the ministry. Brian survived the year without major casualty and would have stayed another, but an interdepartmental mix-up in Kingstown delayed the extension of his permit to work on Bequia as an alien. Our minister of the cloth was unceremoniously escorted aboard the Friendship Rose, with a police sergeant on either arm, to depart Bequia forever.

Luckily the season was over, and the hotel closed for the summer. That gave Karl six months to replace Brian. He entered an ad in the prestigious *Saturday Review*. Most interesting of the responses came from a couple living in the Finger Lakes area of New York. Ellen was, at that time, public relations director for Wells College, a well-known eastern girls' college. Sam was photographer for the college. They lived on a dairy farm which Sam operated, so they understood problems of rural life. Ellen's family had arrived on the Mayflower. Both were bright and involved with education. Karl hired them immediately as we breathed a sigh of relief at the successful solution to our problem.

Spring Hotel opened in November with a long list of bookings. Ellen interviewed and selected a staff. Things were well in hand as we departed for Iowa. The staff discovered early that the new manager was not running a hotel of fun and games. Some changes were good, some bad to our notion, but we stayed out of both the problems and problem solving. Nonetheless, whenever we appeared on the island, Karl was immediately deluged with requests for meetings which never materialized. In earlier days the maids had always sung in the kitchen as they worked. To us, their lilting voices were charming. Ellen stopped the singing, a real loss in our opinion.

Another Bequia tradition Ellen stopped was "toting." Fish heads had previously been available for taking home at night, as well as all leftover food. Obviously that meant twice as much food as was necessary for guests was prepared and carried home. No more! Fish heads were used for soup stock! Staff had a weekly food allowance, purchasing and consuming their own food. Cupboards were fitted with locks so that hotel supplies no longer walked away in tote bags. One morning after this order was well underway, Ellen came down to find signs all over the kitchen — "De Mistress is mean." The culprit author wasn't identified.

We had, as head cook, a pleasant and motherly lady. In addition to being a fine cook, Verna could read as well as was able to double or triple recipes. When the second cook was on duty and making cakes or bread or whatever, it was a case of mixing up a recipe for four plus four plus four until the proper number was reached. Local schools left much to be desired.

Because of frequent plumbing problems at the hotel, Mr. Peavy was often around. We secretly called him "Sweet Pea," because he always smiled sweetly when he was talking to us. In truth he was a hellfire and brimstone lay preacher who had never liked us or anyone at Spring Hotel.

All four rooms at the Gull were occupied when Mr. Peavy was summoned to take care of a plug in one of the toilets. The cleanout was below the road and Mr. Peavy had brought along his "snake." He instructed Ellen to tell guests in all the rooms not to use the toilets. Three were so advised with a note left in a conspicuous spot for the absent one. Naturally that guest returned, missed the note and used the toilet. Mr. Peavy, at that moment, had his face directly in front of the now clear cleanout pipe. A mighty roar echoed across the valley! *"Who shit?"*

Senator Joe McCarthy's assistant and fair-haired lackey, during the communist witch hunts of the 50s, was Roy Cohn. Bright but amoral, he took every advantage to further his public image, no matter at what cost to his adversary's life or reputation. Mr. Cohn disappeared from the national political forum after his tactics fell into disfavor, but he was making money somewhere. At least he had enough to visit Bequia in his large yacht. Deciding he was bored with shipboard life, he booked into Spring Hotel where he and his crew wined and dined for two weeks. One day, without a word, they were gone from the hotel and the island — without payment! Several months later, the captain returned to Bequia. Ellen sought him out and demanded payment. The captain's response was, "Well, I'll tell Mr. Cohn, but I'm surely not paying the bill."

After a barrage of letters, it was finally paid.

The Van Pattens were with us for four years. Then Sam suffered a Bequia induced nervous breakdown which necessitated transfer to St. Vincent civilization. Ellen went with him, weary of cooking when the second cook didn't appear for breakfast, or coping when Sylvia chased the salad man through the filled dining room brandishing a cutlass. She was a Carib and had a temper. The "excitement" was just too much for Sam and Ellen to bear any longer.

So we were on the lookout for another manager.

This time around, it was Dad's selection turn. At the State Bar Convention, he visited with a fellow lawyer about our exotic Caribbean enterprise. A week later we received a call from Sue Hanson from Indiana. With that call began the worst year in the short history of Spring Hotel. Sue drove to Vinton for a personal interview. Blue eyes, with gorgeous red hair and a pleasant personality, she seemed a great possibility. Sue had graduated from Harvard with a B.A. degree and had partially finished the Master's program in history. But that was on hold. For the past year she had run the dining room at a well known resort hotel in Aspen, Colorado. Karl called her former employer and received a glowing recommendation.

We rubbed our hands together in glee and looked forward to a tourist season with the perfect manager. We sent "Red" her ticket and saw her off at the airport. Five days later a cable arrived from Bequia. Sue was in the hospital at

Barbados with a concussion received when she totaled Spring's new Land Rover as she was driving to the harbor — FAST. We telephoned to learn she was in stable condition but would be hospitalized for at least three weeks. In the meantime, we had hotel bookings for the first week in November. However, a college friend of Red's had accompanied her on the plane and could be pressed into temporary service for a month without the requisite work permit. Six weeks later, Sue was still hospitalized. Cassie continued to run the hotel to the satisfaction of the guests. Only 50 percent of the hotel linens were bounced out along the road as Cassie raced to and from the laundress's home in Port Elizabeth. The season limped on from bad to worse after Sue returned to Bequia. In the spring we gave Red her notice…withholding two-months wages to force her into starting and finishing the hotel books for the year. Since November, they'd been tossed into a box. No bills had been paid! She was finally coerced into closeting herself in the Hawksnest. Two weeks later she emerged and handed the books to our accountant. Since we were a year behind on records, Red was long gone when we learned that Spring Hotel was unique in the Caribbean. It had the only bar whose gross sales were exceeded by the cost of the liquor. There were two postscripts to the Hanson year. She took up with a handsome young American and lived with him on his yacht. We heard he beat her regularly and knocked out two of her front teeth.

The second postscript was within our knowledge. Karl got a call from a former lawyer and friend to whom he'd told stories of our Caribbean adventures. Greg had become dean of a large Law School. After preliminary conversation he queried: "Have you heard of a woman named Sue Hanson?"

Karl's hackles rose along with his blood pressure. "You bet I have. Why?"

"Well, I have her application for Law School. Her grades are borderline. She mentions she was manager of a resort hotel on a small Caribbean island. I thought it might be Bequia."

"Darned right it was, Greg. More than that it was our hotel. Greg, if you admit that unprincipled woman to Law School, the good name of the profession will be set back at least ten years."

After the bad year of Sue Hanson's management, we thought perhaps we could find someone we knew to manage the hotel. Johnny Merkel had grown up under our watchful eye. We had visited and vacationed with his family since Johnny was born. We saw him through childhood pranks, and his marriage to his local sweetheart. They were living in California when his mother told him of our latest search. They applied, were interviewed, hired and flew off to Bequia full of enthusiasm for their new adventure. By the end of the season, both had decided the Caribbean was lovely but not for long term and not for working. They returned stateside to a regular life and we were looking again.

With the summer of 1974, former travails ended. Ann Joshua had been managing the Cobblestone Hotel in St. Vincent where her husband was employed by Barclays Bank. When Bong was transferred to Bequia as Barclays manager there, Ann and their young son, Peter, came along. Having learned Ann might be available to manage Spring Hotel, we visited her on Bequia to make inquiry.

Ann was and is intelligent, perceptive, efficient and beautiful. From an old and respected Vincentian family she, as well as her brothers and sisters, was a successful achiever. For two seasons, life ran smoothly at Spring Hotel. There were no staff problems; the food was good; the coconut lowlands were kept clean; guests were happy, and we were ecstatic. In December of 1975, John separated from the service after a three year stint in the U.S. Navy. Since he couldn't enter Law School until September of '76, the three of us thought it a fine idea for him to spend the rest of that season in Bequia learning about the hotel and plantation. He lived at our home on Crown Point until May, the end of the season, then flew back to Iowa.

We lost Ann that May. Bong's advancement brought transfer again and the three of them moved back to St. Vincent where he became a vice president for Barclays.

For those past several years, we had been advertising for buyers of Spring Hotel. We made at least four trips to Bequia with "serious" prospects, all of whom turned out to be flakes or adventurous dreamers. After Ann left we closed the hotel, leaving Sydney Joseph, an assistant Ann had brought with her from the Cobblestone in 1974. Sydney kept an eye on things until 1978 when our promised ten years of indenture for Pioneer Status had expired. We were now free to sell the hotel and get on with our original dream. And in February of 1978, we did.

APPOINTMENT

I'll meet you under the almond tree........
Not beneath the clock at Grand Central........
Not close by the timepiece at Marshall Fields.........
I'll meet you at a timeless timepiece........
A shady place of rest........or work..........as the case may be.
There you can mend a sail.......and leave it for its owner.
There you can leave a message........or start a rumor, or listen.
The very old and the very young,
The wise and the foolish
Gather under the almond tree
Any day.......on a magic island.

March 11, 1967

Bob and Arnold

BOB AND ARNOLD

Bob and Arnold had been friends for a long time. As engineers, they thought alike. They trusted each other. They enjoyed the same things. Now, they, with their wives, were vacationing on Bequia.

The trip almost had been aborted. Arnold had scheduled a cataract operation which, in the 1960s, meant no lifting or jarring for a month, but after the surgery and after the blessings and admonitions of Arnold's doctor, the two couples had flown to the Caribbean.

Bequia was a great place for R and R. Soon Arnold was eager for activity. The first project was the construction of a "changing house" on Spring Beach for American vacationers unwilling to use available bushes. The two engineers spent a whole day putting together a base of barbed wire (borrowed from somewhere) into which was woven a dried thatch of palm fronds that reached head high from the sand. It was splendid and all applauded the innovative engineers.

With no repercussions from that activity, Arnold queried Bob about a packetboat trip to the mainland the next day. The two of them left on the daily boat at 6:30 a.m. They did not return on the only afternoon boat from St. Vincent that was to arrive in Bequia at 4:45 p.m. Instead, at about dinner time, the bedraggled duo plodded into the Sunny Caribbee where we were all staying. This was their story.

Bob had wanted to get two Royal Palm trees for his friend Karl. They had gone to the Botanical Gardens and made the purchase, but because of the relaxed attitude of the garden director and their taxi driver, they had missed the return boat. Bob, always resourceful, walked the beach until he found someone willing to rent a small sailing canoe to the two of them. The boat was to be collected in Bequia by the owner the following day.

Bob was a master sailor but was concerned with Arnold's physical problems in the event of a dunking. So, before they cast off, he rigged a life jacket for Arnold. It consisted of two lengths of old bamboo found on the beach — one in front, one in back — laced together with a length of rope found on the beach, and then tied under Arnold's shoulders. Thus reassured, the two set off. With wind and current behind them, their sleigh-ride on a canoe made of a hollowed-out log was both daring and exciting. Both were glad to round the headland and sail into Admiralty Bay. As they neared the harbor, Arnold, realizing his need for his security blanket was over, removed the improvised life jacket and tossed it over the gunwale. Incredulously, they watched as the "life jacket" gurgled its way through the clear Caribbean waters to the sand on the bottom of the bay.

MAXIM

WATERLOGGED BAMBOO DOESN'T FLOAT.

THE NOVICE

The rest of the party assembled at O'Hare Field for the long flight to Bequia, but Charlie had a medical meeting in Miami, so he, Marilyn and his scuba tank were scheduled to join us in San Juan. Charlie, being efficient, had his scuba tank filled before the Miami-San Juan flight, and it was only when we were checking in for the next leg of the journey that he learned filled tanks on planes were a dangerous *no-no*. He was alerted to the fact most emphatically by airline personnel, who suggested that he empty the tank — *immediately.* Where would you go to empty a scuba tank if you were in an airport? Charlie allowed as how an unoccupied corner would be perfect. He loosened the valve and all the banshees of hell began to shriek as that compressed air was freed. It was a job which, once begun, could not be stopped. A few minutes later, a red-faced young doctor reported back to the airline check-in counter. We all pretended he was a stranger.

YUL TARZAN

He exists only in my memory today, but in the 1960s Jack Lindsey was definitely an island character. The nickname was my own…"Yul" for his polished baldness, "Tarzan" for his barefoot, bare-chested appearance, with a snow-white, diaper-like garment as a concession to society. He lived on his Bequia built boat in the harbor. Stories abounded about Jack's former life, and he always added another during our infrequent conversations. One, that he was a former member of a prestigious midwestern ballet

company, seemed plausible, for he was lithe and quick as a cat exhibiting his dancing skills at every island Jump-Up.

Jack didn't like people. Caustic insults won few friends. He made the rounds of local hotels and restaurants, leaving each at the request of the manager who refused to tolerate the contempt he showed guests. After several months, he was back again, but again the ban was soon enforced.

An example of exhibitionism was the sharpened swordfish bone he tucked into the waistline of his shorts, always prominently displayed.

One evening after an hour of frenetic Caribbean dancing at a local night spot, Jack sank breathless to the floor, automatically crossing his legs in a favorite position, but gyrations had misplaced the dagger. It jabbed into his groin, producing a bloody wound. Despite pleas, Jack refused to visit the clinic for an antibiotic and returned to his boat in Admiralty Bay. After three days another yachtsman checked on the state of his health. Jack lay delirious and bloated in his bunk. He was immediately transferred to the hospital, but peritonitis had set in. Jack Lindsey was dead by nightfall, his own victim.

FRED WAGNER

My first glimpse of Fred Wagner was in the mid-60s when we were staying at the Sunny Caribbee. In a high pitched, strident voice, he berated his wife as the rest of us looked on — embarrassed. Minutes later he introduced himself in a high pitched, sweet voice. Fred was a tall, balding man. Through some chicanery he had bought Industry, just beyond Spring, so that we frequently saw him walking to or from the harbor always clad in immaculate Bermuda length white shorts and white cuffed knee socks and using a walking stick. We always spoke, of course, but I had difficulty erasing my first impression of Fred.

After Spring Hotel opened, we started developing the hills in accordance with the requirement of our Aliens' License. With homes being added each year, we thought it would be a real selling point to bring electricity to the windward side of Bequia. Even then some foreigners were reluctant to forego the advantages of electric living, and we felt its addition would increase lot sales.

John Gold, one of our lot owners from Barbados, was Chairman of the Board of the Caribbean Development Corporation, in charge of power for all the islands. John induced the local manager to give us a bid for the project which would include bringing power poles and lines from Thomas Hill, a long distance and great expense.

At about the same time, Fred drew up development plans for Windward Island Plantation, the new name for Industry. It was our feeling that we two developers should cooperate by sharing the cost of any electric project benefitting us both. Karl's stateside experience had been that agreement should be made before work was started and before those further out merely hooked on to what we had already financed.

When Karl learned of Fred's arrival on Bequia and residence at "Retreat," a private home perched on a cliff above the harbor, he sent a letter by cab driver and requested an appointment two days later at Retreat to discuss such a project. But the cab driver put the return note in his pocket and promptly forgot to deliver it until Thursday morning, well past Wednesday afternoon's meeting time. In that reply, Fred had responded that he was busy on Wednesday afternoon and couldn't see Karl.

Receiving no message, Karl assumed that all was "go" and knocked at Retreat's door on Wednesday afternoon. He was shown in by a lady servant. He found Fred lounging on the veranda, rum punch in hand.

Fred sputtered as he confronted Karl, "I told you I was going to be busy this afternoon."

Karl responded, "Fred, I received no message at all."

"Well, I'm not interested," countered Fred. "If you want to put in electricity, just put it in." He rose and showed Karl out the door.

What a boor! We'd heard many stories about Fred, among which was one telling of a small bell at his place at dinner when entertaining. Not to summon the maid, ringing of the bell signaled that conversation should cease as "Fred the Great" wished to speak. This was another example of the total lack of civility to anyone he felt to be his social inferior.

Without Industry's contribution, costs were prohibitive, so we continued to use our propane and kerosene lamps.

Several years later, Windward Island Plantation employed Martin Price, a very personable young Englishman with Caribbean experience, to promote the project. Several condominiums were built on speculation. One was sold to Ann Blair, an acquaintance of ours, who mentioned that her contract included electricity being furnished to her. A week later Karl received a note from Fred requesting a meeting at Industry's beach house. Fred, of course, had no idea we had learned the specifics of Ann's contract.

"Karl, I was wrong in refusing to bring electricity out here. You were right about this being a proper time. I surely want to go along with your proposal."

Without hesitation, Karl answered, "Fred, we've reconsidered. It's just too expensive. We're well organized at Spring and have decided we don't want to change the hotel's charm with electricity."

Fred leaped out of his chair, knocking it over in his haste. He shrieked, "But, Karl, you need it. You need it!!!"

Knowing he held the upper hand, Karl stood up saying, "Well, Fred, if you bring it out, maybe we'll hook on."

As he walked up the road and around Crown Point, Karl could hear Fred reviling him until, finally, his squeaky voice was carried off by the wind.

Next morning, Martin, the diplomat, visited us. "Come on, Karl, let's do this together. We both know you need electricity, too."

"Right, Martin. We'll hook on after Fred brings it out."

"Please! Please, Karl!"

And so, Karl capitulated. Spring and Industry would share costs from Thomas Hill to the Spring boundary. Spring would pay for installation from there to the northern boundary and Industry could carry it wherever they wanted from there. Martin told Fred. Fred said, "Fine."

That is how electricity came to the windward coast of Bequia!

AUTHORITIES

Our son, John, having been discharged in December, 1975, after three years of reorganizing the United States Navy, decided it would be a good time to get a little practical experience. So he planned to spend the winter on Bequia representing management, pending the sale of Spring Hotel.

One of John's highest priorities was cutting brush and beautifying the beach and coconut grove area in the flatland below the hotel. At mid-morning on a sunny February day, he and Sydney Joseph, a friend and employee of Spring Hotel, took a few minutes from their hot work to run some errands in the harbor town of Port Elizabeth...ten minutes away on a sometimes two strip concrete road. John was shirtless, wearing shorts and work boots. Sydney was likewise sartorially perfect in shorts, sneakers and a sweat-streaked T-shirt. As the two rounded the corner on Bay Street, one of the young postal employees hailed them.

"Mr. Fischer, you have a package in the post office."

Because such an event looms large on Bequia, John and Sydney pulled to the side of the street, where John hopped out of the Land Rover and ran across to collect his package, arriving at the same moment as the young postal employee who slipped behind the counter and questioned, in his official capacity, "What can I do for you?"

Unbelieving, John countered, "You just told me I have a package, I'd like to get it."

"Mr. Fischer, you can't come in here without a shirt."

"But I only want to collect my package."

"Mr. Fischer, you must have a shirt."

John re-crossed the street to Sydney, waiting in the Rover.

"Do you have any identification?"

"Identification? You know who I am. You just called me Mr. Fischer. Why do I need identification?"

"Hey, Sydney, can I borrow your shirt? They won't give me my package this way."

Sydney pulled off his wet shirt and offered it to John, who put it on and returned to the post office where the same young postal employee was at the window.

"Fine. What can I do for you?"

"I have a package."

"Oh, yes, a package. And what is your name?"

"You know my name. I come in here every day."

"What is your name, please?"

"John Fischer."

"Do you have any identification?"

"Identification? You know who I am. You just called me Mr. Fischer. Why do I need identification?"

"Do you have identification, please?"

John's habit was to carry his wallet at all times to avoid it walking away in his absence. He shuffled through its contents, coming up with an outdated naval identification card which he proffered. It was carefully examined and returned to him.

"Yes, you seem to be John Fischer."

"Well, then, may I have my package?"

"I must open the package for customs and duty examination before I give it to you."

Done. A duty of $20.00 levied. Twenty dollars paid over. Package received. The contents? A bedraggled and denuded Christmas tree complete with tiny ornaments and bearing the return address of Michelle Paulos, John's future wife.

DON MAIZE

Don Maize became our good neighbor in the 80s when he bought and renovated the Pope house just below us. We told him many of our early-day stories during twilight visits at one house or the other. When we chuckled about John's experience with the mails and his Christmas tree, Don offered one of his own.

Don was becoming a permanent resident of Bequia, but it was still necessary to visit the post office to fill out the proper form for visa extension. He queued up one morning, and after an hour of waiting, he worked his way to the front of the line and requested the form. It and a pen were shoved to him. Don filled out the form and returned it to the clerk, who took one look and refused to extend.

"Why do you refuse?" asked Don. "This is the way I've always done it."

"Well, Mr. Maize, you have used the wrong color of ink in your application."

"But," insisted Don, "I wrote it with the pen you just gave me."

"Nonetheless," retorted the young man, "you must write it with the proper color of ink."

Bureaucracy!!!!!

SECOND HOME

And because you have never visited the tropics,
    you question
But how does one decorate a West Indian home?
So I would answer........well, as for me

I have a floor carpeted multicolor. It is mauve and cerise
    bougainvillea.
Blossoms loosed by the winds to bloom again beneath my
    feet.
Open walls offer four murals for my approval.......
Each an original by the master artist.
The first, a fringe of white sand, blue waters and a cauldron
    of boiling reef surf.
The second, a twin. of islands hazy in the distance…
    …soft in sunlight, forboding in rain.
To my right a hummingbird's nest of aquamarine water,
A deep bay with a nesting of white froth and one small
    fishing-boat egg.
Finally, freckles spotting a green hillside.......Other homes,
    like ours, filled with those seeking the reality of a dream.

And table decorations, you ask?

My favorite is a pair of tiny sugar birds.
Yellow and black, they flitter from table to chair to
    swinging lamp,
Where they loudly consider its possibilities as this year's
    nest.......disappearing through the openwork, only to
    reappear with further chittering.

At breakfast tomorrow they will join us, bringing grass and
    string and soft stuffs
Which will fall out the lamp's bottom — piece by piece
    by piece.
A symphony of music fills my hilltop home.

The constant background of the trade winds
With surf timpani rising to a storm crescendo
And a changing melody of mocking birds and Bequia
    sweets.

But you understand.......this is only for today and only
    for me.
Someone else would have his own lares and penates.

March, 1978

A "TELLING" OF TASTE

RECIPES

This is a "telling" of Caribbean flavors. Quantities and some of the other specifics are your choice and inclination — island style. All of these recipes were built around ingredients available on Bequia...lobster from the sea, eggs from the back yard chickens, fresh vegetables, local lamb. Other things come and go with the boats or availability on neighboring islands. Today the Rastafarians grow wonderful vegetables on St. Vincent, as do other locals. Baking powder, yeast and curry, come in plastic bags.

GREEN FOOD

Until we lived in the tropics, I didn't know about picking green bananas, green paw-paw and green tomatoes. I soon learned that all ripen in a day or two. If not harvested green, they are discovered by birds or manicoos and consumed with gusto.

BEQUIA CHEESE PUFF

Use a medium-size greased casserole. Butter bread, take off crusts and cut into finger slices. Make a layer of bread, then chopped onion, then grated cheese. Sprinkle in a few drops of hot pepper sauce, salt and pepper. Repeat layers till dish is full. Beat 3 eggs with 1 1/2 cups milk (enough to just cover bread). Beat in 1 Tablespoon prepared mustard. Pour over bread and soak at least 1 hour or till bread has absorbed a lot of the moisture. Bake at 350° for 1/2 to 3/4 hour or till crisp and brown on top.

CARIB EGGS

Halve 8 hard-cooked eggs. Remove yokes, mash and season with salt, mustard, cream and 1/2 cup grated cheddar cheese. Fill egg whites with mixture and put eggs in shallow baking dish. Heat 1 can stewed tomatoes with onion and green pepper and a little butter. Pour over eggs, add more grated cheese. Bake at 400° for 15 minutes or till hot.

LOBSTER NEWBURG

1 cup butter or margarine, melted
3 lbs. lobster, chunked
12 tablespoons cornstarch
2 teaspoons salt
1/4 teaspoon cayenne pepper (more if you like it hotter)
2 teaspoons paprika
2 Tablespoons Worcestershire sauce
3 cups milk
2 cups cream (if none, milk is OK)
1 cup sherry

On low heat, add lobster chunks to butter and stir till well coated. Add cornstarch and stir till well blended. Add other seasonings, then add milk and cream, stirring constantly. When mixture has thickened, add sherry slowly. Blend. Serve over toast points or rice.

FISH PIE

Flake 1 1/2 pounds of any kind of poached whitefish. Chop 1 medium-size onion and chives (about 1 tablespoon), 1 green pepper and 2 tomatoes. Brown lightly in butter or margarine. Make a medium-thick cream sauce. Add salt and pepper to taste and pour over flaked fish. Beat 2 eggs and add to mixture, mixing together. Cover with 2 riced potatoes, dot with butter. Bake uncovered at 350° till brown on top.

BILIN'S (Boilings)
(This is messy looking but good.)
Poach any whitefish, skin and flake. Add cubed potatoes, carrots and onions. Add hot sauce to flavor. Add enough water to cook for a long time without sticking.

BEEF OR LAMB CURRY

2 lbs. meat, cubed
1 cup water with 2 beef bouillon cubes
1 can tomato paste or equal amount fresh tomatoes
1/2 teaspoon grated fresh ginger
1 clove garlic (or more) diced
1 teaspoon salt
1/2 teaspoon pepper
1 teaspoon Worcestershire sauce
2 Tablespoons (or more) curry powder
1/2 cup grated coconut
1/4 cup seedless raisins
2 tart apples
one large onion, diced
1 teaspoon dried parsley

Place all ingredients in large, covered stew kettle. Bring to boil, reduce heat and cook till meat is tender. Stir occasionally and add water if it begins to stick. Should end as a thick sauce. Serve over hot rice. Add **"Boys"** (condiments) in separate bowls...to top off curry and rice.

BOYS (condiments)

Cut up fresh tomatoes, chopped green pepper, chopped onion, chopped ripe olives, chopped hard-cooked eggs, chopped peanuts, chopped celery, farina, crumbled fried bacon, bananas chopped or sliced and mixed with brown sugar, candied ginger, shredded coconut, paw paw or cantaloupe cubed, small pickled onions, chutney, chopped green onions, mixed pickled cauliflower relish, and whatever else you might think of. Each has its own bowl.

"Boys" comes from India when the Brits were there. Each boy (servant) would carry in a separate condiment for the curry. More "boys" indicated more wealth.

EGGPLANT FRITTERS

1 small eggplant, peeled and cubed
1 beaten egg
1 small onion, grated
salt and pepper
1/3 cup flour
1 teaspoon baking powder
2 Tablespoons milk or tomato sauce

Cook eggplant in 1/4 cup water till tender. Drain well and mash. Stir in egg, onion, salt and pepper. Mix flour and baking powder and stir into mixture. Add enough milk to make a drop batter. Drop by spoonfuls into shallow cooking oil and cook till brown on both sides.

CABBAGE CASSEROLE

Arrange 1 cabbage, sliced, cooked and drained well in a buttered casserole. Add 1 chopped onion, 1 can undiluted cream of mushroom soup, cubed cheddar cheese to taste. Top with buttered crumbs. Bake uncovered at 350° till brown.

CHEESED CHRISTOPHENE

(Christophene is known in the US as chayote. It is in the summer squash family.)

Underwater, peel and cube christophene. Layer in a buttered casserole, adding onion slices at intervalsMake a thick cheese sauce and pour over all. Top with buttered crumbs. Bake uncovered at 350° for 45 minutes or till brown.

BANANAS CARIBBEAN

4 bananas
1/2 cup brown sugar
1/2 cup orange juice
1/4 cup nutmeg
1/4 cup cinnamon
1/2 cup sherry
1 Tablespoon butter
2 Tablespoons rum
heavy cream

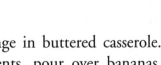

Split bananas lengthwise, arrange in buttered casserole. Combine and heat other ingredients, pour over bananas. Bake till tender. Remove and sprinkle with rum. Serve with cream.

COCONUT CRUNCH

1 cup ground graham crackers, vanilla wafers,
   or something similar
1 cup shredded coconut
1/2 cup chopped nuts
4 egg whites
salt
1 teaspoon vanilla
1 cup sugar

Mix crumbs, coconut and nuts. Beat egg whites, salt and vanilla till foamy. Add sugar gradually and beat till stiff like meringue. Fold in dry mixture. Pour into 8- or 9-inch square pan. Bake at 350° for 30 minutes. Cool and top with ice cream if available.

BANANA COCONUT BREAD

1 cup sugar
1/3 cup butter or margarine
1/2 cup mashed bananas
2 cups flour
4 teaspoons baking powder
1 teaspoon salt
1/2 teaspoon soda
2 eggs, well beaten
3 tablespoons milk
1/2 cup grated coconut

Cream sugar and shortening, add mashed bananas. Sift flour with baking powder, salt and soda. Add to first mixture alternately with egg and milk mixture. Stir in coconut, add peanuts if desired. Bake in 300° oven about 1 1/4 hours.

EPILOGUE
1997

Today, with second owners, tiny Spring Hotel flourishes for escapists and brags about its Sunday curry dinners with three or more sittings. The key lime and rum pies made fresh from the plantation ingredients are luscious as ever. Karl still works on the development of Spring Plantation which has become a charming community of international residents: doctors, lawyers, musicians, engineers, authors, and business men and women running the gamut (second homes to others who wanted a "little bit of the Caribbean" for their own).

Bequia has changed dramatically since we first stepped ashore. Its "James F. Mitchell" airport is up-to-date, admits small jets and regularly scheduled airlines make daily stops. Ferry service to St. Vincent is provided four times daily by several companies with large steel-hulled boats. Nearly all roads are paved with concrete for the hundreds of cars and trucks used on the island.

Sailors the world over are still discovering Bequia's snug harbor in the paradise of the Windward Islands. Two to three hundred sailboats of all kinds and shapes rattle their chains at anchorage every night. Their gleaming masts and shiny fiber-glassed hulls stand out in sharp contrast to the wooden inter-island schooners probably built on Bequia during or before our early years.

A dozen or so cruise ships a week, many looking like small battleships, disgorge their passengers into gigs that line the shores and docks of Port Elizabeth.

From no communications at all, the island progressed to radio telephone, then to a modern telephone system with direct dial to the States and Europe and, for some, to satellite telephone systems. St. Vincent has enjoyed a television station and two modern FM radio stations for years now. The hillsides are dotted with TV dishes. The island is filled with computers and E-mail afficionados.

At night, lights in the Port Elizabeth hills display the modern homes not dreamed about ten years before. We still remember the dim pinpoints of the kerosene lamps that hinted at civilization in those hills. With the installation of diesel generators years ago, the kerosene lamps, hung high on poles along the bay, disappeared and the lamplighters became extinct. So did the bait fishermen, who, on dark nights, sailed their little double-ended boats back and forth across the bay, brilliant torches held high, seining for ballyhoo.

Some of the old ways still exist. Whale watching for the whalers of Bequia is still done. As recently as the spring of 1997, as in the olden days, the sole whaleboat raced after three whales that were sighted, but it was unsuccessful.

Bequia's annual Easter Regatta chums in sailboats from neighboring islands. Races of the little double-ended boats are thrilling and competition keen; even the Bequia children vie for honors in racing tiny boats made of coconut husks.

Rum remains the drink of choice and is freely consumed. (When we first arrived, a fifth of rum was selling for less than a bottle of Coke. That has changed.) Limes are still squeezed and bottled in old rum bottles; peanuts roasted and bottled in beer bottles. Brooms are still made of wild grasses bound with twine. Anglican weddings continue the island tradition of wrapping the priest's stole over joined hands of bride and groom, and many couples still wait until birth of the second or third child before that stole is wrapped.

Today the drawbacks are few and the rewards many on that tiny island in the middle of a very large Caribbean Sea.